# The Concept of the Trinity Is Not Biblical

by
Allen Nance

**RoseDog Books**
PITTSBURGH, PENNSYLVANIA 15238

The contents of this work, including, but not limited to, the accuracy of events, people, and places depicted; opinions expressed; permission to use previously published materials included; and any advice given or actions advocated are solely the responsibility of the author, who assumes all liability for said work and indemnifies the publisher against any claims stemming from publication of the work.

All Rights Reserved
Copyright © 2022 by Allen Nance

No part of this book may be reproduced or transmitted, downloaded, distributed, reverse engineered, or stored in or introduced into any information storage and retrieval system, in any form or by any means, including photocopying and recording, whether electronic or mechanical, now known or hereinafter invented without permission in writing from the publisher.

RoseDog Books
585 Alpha Drive, Suite 103
Pittsburgh, PA 15238
Visit our website at *www.rosedogbookstore.com*

ISBN: 979-8-88527-536-1
ESIBN: 979-8-88527-586-6

# Preface

In religious circles the normal system of education is missing two important components; research and verification. The most common teaching process is simple. I am going to teach you what I was taught. Whatever I say, you accept it as the truth; then you go teach it to the next group. We trust that those who came before us got it right. We have no need to confirm, verify, or challenge what has been passed down through the centuries.

The truth is, there are several ideas that are taught as doctrine that cannot be taught directly from scripture. During the Protestant Reformation, many of the Roman Catholic Church's practices where challenged. Martin Luther, John Calvin, and others did what they could to put Christian behavior back in the forefront. Many Catholic practices were outright rejected. Unfortunately, as some of the new churches were forming, they continued with some Catholic Doctrine.

Printed texts were not as plentiful as they are today. The majority of the Bibles at that time were owned by the clergy of the church. The people had no choice but to accept what they were taught by the church leaders as being the truth and accurate. The Roman Catholic Church had great influence throughout Europe. To avoid having a political conflict within England, King Henry VIII made himself head of the church. When it came to religious decisions, he deliberately chose to maintain Catholic doctrine. Although the Church of England was considered Protestant, they were still teaching Roman Catholic ideals. Other Protestant churches made some of the same decisions.

A few of those non-biblical, Roman Catholic-created doctrine are still being taught in Protestant churches today. We cannot use lack of printed Bibles as the excuse. As stated earlier, we just teach what we have been taught. We do not search the Bible to verify doctrine before we teach it. The teaching of the Trinity (God the Father, God the Son, and God the Holy Spirit) is one doctrine that cannot be found directly in scripture. It may be better said, scripture does not teach the Trinity as doctrine. Support for the false doctrine is found by picking and choosing certain verses.

All quotes in this work are from the King James Version (KJV) of the Holy Bible. The primary reason is it has been the most widely used English translation for many years. It is also the English translation that is used most often to support Trinity teaching. The history of the KJV is that it was translated directly from the Hebrew and Greek Biblical text. The King's reason for commissioning the translation into English was personal and political. However, he sent translators to the original language texts so he could claim to have the most accurate English translation. That still leaves the question, did the New Testament (NT) translators make an effort to be sure they had the most accurate Greek version to translate from? Also, did the Old Testament (OT) translators actually use a Hebrew language text or a Greek translation of the OT?

There are other good English translations available. But a few of the modern versions would more appropriately be described as interpretations. Some of them were written for ease of reading, for style of expression, or to interpret scripture to express a certain understanding.

Many teachers choose the translation that expresses a passage the way they want their students to understand it. Some will actually use a different translation for a different lesson. At times, several different translations are used within the same lesson. That can be a useful method for reaching a true understanding. However, within any one lesson it is important to use one primary translation for the purpose of consistency. When discussing doctrine, the chosen translation should be as close to the original language text, the God-inspired text, as is reasonably possible. Due to the influence of previous translations, teaching, and theology of the day, there are translation errors in the KJV. That may be true for any translation. However, for the sake of consistency, only the one translation will be used as the primary in this work.

Again, the KJV is the most widely used English translation for teaching the Trinity. Using it as the primary in this work eliminates the excuse, when conflicts are found, that using different translations is the only reason. Other translations will be quoted in a few instances to express the true meaning of certain verses. However, most scriptural conflicts with Trinity teaching will be shown to exist between the doctrine and the very translation used to teach it. The truth will be revealed.

# Table of Contents

Preface  *(Why this book is needed)* .......................... iii

Let's Do a Little Housekeeping ........................ 1
*(Important things to consider before reading this book)*

The Doctrine; The Trinity ............................ 7
*(What the doctrine is and how it became a Christian doctrine)*

How is Scripture Applied ............................ 15
*(The study of scripture that is used to teach the doctrine)*

    There is Only One God ........................... 16

    One God Consists of Three Persons ................ 19

    Three Persons of God are ........................ 27
    Distinguished One from Another

    Each Member of the Trinity is God ................ 35

        The Father is God ........................... 35

        The Holy Spirit is God ....................... 37

        The Son is God ............................. 38

        The Study of John 1:1–18 .................... 53

Why We Should Not Teach or Accept the Trinity as Doctrine . . . 67

    Why we should not teach or believe in "God the Son" .... 69

    Why you should not believe in "God the Holy Spirit" .... 72

Conclusion ....................................... 75

# Let's do a Little Housekeeping

Before we begin a discussion about an accepted doctrine of the church, we must first establish the foundation on which all doctrine should be based. 2 Timothy 3:16 reads:

*All scripture is given by inspiration of God, and is profitable for doctrine, for reproof, for correction, for instruction in righteousness:* If the teaching of the Trinity is to be accepted as a true Doctrine of Christianity, there should be God-inspired scripture that makes that statement directly. While looking for the proof, we must be careful not to read into scripture what we were first taught or what we want it to say. A common habit of people, when looking for proof of something they already believe to be true, is to overlook verses that do not fit into what they think they know. It is difficult for most to objectively read familiar scripture. We are often taught something that has been passed down through the years. Then we are given a few verses to read that we are told supports what we were taught. When we read the given scripture, we automatically see exactly what we were looking for. That is the very case in the teaching of the Trinity.

Most people will resist a teacher who tells them what they have believed all of their life is not the truth. That is when we must go back to scripture to help us with "reproof," "correction," and "instruction in righteousness." We should begin by reminding them what scripture says about the attributes of a wise man.

*Proverbs 1:5*
*A wise man will hear, and will increase learning; and a man of understanding shall attain unto wise counsels:*

*Proverbs 9:8–9*
*Reprove not a scorner, lest he hate thee: rebuke a wise man, and he will love thee. Give instruction to a wise man, and he will be yet wiser: teach a just man, and he will increase in learning.*

A person who truly wants to be seen as righteous will, in most cases, also wish to be considered spiritually wise. The desire to be wise will create in them a willingness to listen to, and hopefully learn from, something that may increase their knowledge. Many people confuse being smart with being wise. That person will think the truth could only be what they already know. They may display anger if they are told otherwise. For those who have the right attitude, we can go back to scripture to give them another reason to be willing to listen and learn.

*Hebrews 5:12*
*For when for the time ye ought to be teachers, ye have need that one teach you again which be the first principles of the oracles of God; and are become such as have need of milk, and not of strong meat.*

Even as adults we should always be eager to be taught something new. As a Christian, having an open mind to learning is "the first principles of the oracles of God." You may wonder why, as adults, we are in need of learning the very basics ("have need of milk"). At some point in our childhood, we have probably all played the story game. All of the students in the class were put in a line. The teacher whispered a statement to the first person and

## The Concept of the Trinity Is Not Biblical

told them to quickly whisper it to the person behind them. By the time it reached the last person in line, the statement had change noticeably. The same has happened over the years in the church. As different teachers, with different motives and interpretations, through different generations, have passed down explanations of scripture, some of the original meanings and understanding have gotten lost. Some of what we think we know today is not what those who recorded God's inspired Word intended it to mean. God, in His wisdom, anticipated this problem. That is why He had Hebrews 5:12 written. We should be willing to be taught again.

Some of the basic milk that we need to be taught again are the very topics we teach in church today as doctrine. As stated earlier, if we are going to be sure we have the correct understanding of what we teach as doctrine, we must first seek the foundation for the teaching in God's Word. The beginning of knowledge and wisdom is the fear of the Lord (Proverbs 1:7, 9:10). The establishment and understanding of true doctrine are the first things the knowledge of scripture profits us. Correction is another profit we get from the proper application of scripture. In the child's game, the teacher made the correction after the last child stated what they thought they were told. The Holy Spirit (Spirit of Truth) will be our teacher. We will be taught again as we re-read scripture with the Spirit's guidance (John 16:13). The Spirit-led understanding will provide the correction. In the process, scripture will prove whether our current understanding of what has been passed down is or is not correct.

It is important to pray that God will give you the guidance of the Holy Spirit as you read scripture. That is how 2 Timothy 2:15 will be fulfilled. "Study to shew thyself approved unto God, a workman that needeth not to be ashamed, rightly dividing the word of truth." Still a good teacher may be needed at times. 2 Peter 3:16 tells us "some things (are) hard to be understood."

If scripture is to be profitable for doctrine, there should be verses that directly teach the concept. When those verses are identified, the explanation and understanding of the verses must not create a conflict with other verses. A great example of this comes in Matthew 4 verses 5 through 7. In the Devil's attempt to test Jesus, he quoted scripture (Psalms 91:11–12). He wanted Jesus to deliberately take a dangerous leap with the pretense the scripture says the angels would save Him. Jesus quickly showed the Devil's understanding of scripture created a conflict with another verse of scripture. He also quoted scripture (Deuteronomy 6:16) to show the fault in the Devil's application of the verses and how it conflicted with other verses. To take Satan's challenge would be testing God. That, we are told not to do. The Devil first decided he wanted Jesus to take his dare. Then he found and quoted scripture to make it seem okay to do so. We must take great care that we do not inadvertently follow the Devil's example. Keep that in mind as we study the Trinity doctrine and the verses of scripture used for its teaching.

It is important that you have the proper understanding of the purpose of this work. It will be shown the doctrine of the Trinity is a commandment of men (Matthew 15:9). The Word of God, as it is applied to Trinity teaching, will be examined and discussed in context for the sole purpose of bringing forth the truth. In no way should any of the discussion cause you to feel the roles Jesus and the Holy Spirit play in your life are diminished or changed. Jesus is, and always will be, the Messiah, the Christ, our Savior, and the Son of God (John 1:41, John 3:16, Matthew 3:17). The Holy Spirit is, and always will be, our Comforter, our teacher, and the Spirit of Truth (John 14:17, 26). Their importance in our lives cannot be reduced because scripture teaches they both are doing the will of He who sent them (GOD). No matter what title we use to refer to them, that fact does not change. However, it will be made plain one of the titles given to Jesus and the Holy Spirit in Trinity teaching, only the Trinity title, contradicts God's written Word. We are

## The Concept of the Trinity Is Not Biblical

to see them, and refer to them, as we are directed in scripture. There is no other God-given guide for us to follow.

In a conversation on the subject, the usual Trinity-support verses were quoted. That was followed with the statement, "We must be able to trust Scripture." That is a very true statement. That is the very reason scripture will be quoted and discussed in context to reveal the truth. What we should, however, be a little leery of are the teachers. Do they apply scripture correctly? What is the source of information used in their understanding and explanation of scripture? What is their true motive and intention when they choose certain verses of scripture? Reading scripture, applying scripture correctly, and gaining the true understanding is the only way scripture will profit us the reproof and correction we seek. Yes, we must be able to trust scripture. That trust will be gained from the true understand we will receive from the Spirit of Truth.

As we study this topic, very important points will be repeated several times. If you do not use the KJV as your daily scripture resource, you should have your favorite translation handy to verify what is written here, for your personal understanding.

Some will ask, why does all of this matter? The primary reason—we are being disobedient to God. God told us not to bow down to anything in Heaven, on Earth, or under the Earth. (Exodus 20:3–5). Some will say this restriction is only toward graven images and likenesses. But verse three says "no other gods." That is not limited to only those we might make statues or pictures of. We rationalize our way around this by saying Jesus and the Holy Spirit are the same God. Therefore, we can pray to them without violating God's instructions. The irony is we are also being disobedient to Jesus. He clearly tells us to pray to the Father in His name. (Matthew 6:6, 6:9, John 15:16, 16:23, etc.) By teaching the Son is God, we have decided for ourselves it is okay to ignore what the Son says. We rationalize Jesus's instructions away also. We say when He says pray to the Father, He is really telling us to pray to

God, meaning Himself. How He said it does not matter to us. But Jesus does not say pray to God. He said pray to the Father. Even in Trinity teaching, Jesus is not the Father. When we pray to Jesus, we are following the commandment of men. Matthew 15:6b "Thus you have made the commandment of God of no effect by your tradition."

This study will show prayer is not the only area we ignore God's Word. The Trinity doctrine has allowed us to say what is written is not what God really meant. We can make our own decisions about what scripture means and how they should be applied. As a matter of fact, that is why the doctrine was adopted. God is not happy with our disobedience.

# The Doctrine
# The Trinity

The doctrine of the Trinity definition: There is one God who exists in three distinct persons. The Father, The Son, and The Holy Spirit are each individual persons but all three are fully God. Using that definition gives license to call each of the persons God. In Trinity teaching they are most often called by the titles God the Father, God the Son, and God the Holy Spirit. The Father is the only one who is directly called God in scripture, yet the doctrine is widely accepted throughout the Christian community. How did the concept of the Trinity become a Christian doctrine?

We must first remember Jesus's entire life and ministry, death, and resurrection took place while the nation of Israel was under Roman rule. Not all of the early Christians were of Hebrew heritage. Many were naturally born Roman citizens (gentiles) who came to believe in Jesus. Others were Roman citizens who were of Hebrew (Jewish) heritage and accepted Roman citizenship for prestige. The Apostle Paul (originally Saul) was one in the group of Hebrew Romans. He accepted Christianity after his conversion on the road to Damascus. He wrote the book of Romans to help with the understanding for those in the gentile group. As the Christian Faith grew, new believers included both Jews and gentiles.

As the new Christian religion spread through the land there was resistance from the unaccepting Jews and persecutions by the Roman Emperors. Roman culture, however, was such that the citizens accepted all forms of religion as long as it did not conflict with the government and its official religion. Remember, Pilot did not find any fault in Jesus. Jesus had not violated any Roman laws. Pilot only ordered the crucifixion because of pressure from the Jewish leaders. He washed his hands of taking any responsibility for Jesus's death. Ironically, that kind of hands-off policy is what allowed Christianity to grow at such a fast pace within the Empire despite the opposition. Yet, some of the emperors that came along after Jesus's resurrection did not like Christians because they only practiced the one religion and worshipped only one God. They wanted the Christians to also follow some of the local religions and show respect to other gods. Not doing so was an insult to the Empire.

Roman history shows there were many religions practiced among its citizens. Each family chose the religions and gods they wanted to worship. However, they were all expected to show respect to the official religion of the Empire. The official religion was the one that was primarily practiced by the current Emperor. Christianity developed strong roots within the Empire, but it took about three hundred years before an Emperor made it the official religion of the Empire. That Emperor was Constantine. Prior to his acceptance of Christianity, Constantine was a sun god worshipper. Some say his mother had accepted Christianity earlier than he. Constantine was converted after seeing the sign of a cross in an awake vision then later in a dream He attributed his leadership successes to that sign.

As the religion grew, gentile Christians were still somewhat influenced by the traditions and religions of old. That is one reason we are warned in scripture not to be spoiled by the "traditions of men." (Colossians 2:8) The desire to maintain traditions created conflicts within the empire. Many citizens wanted to continue the practice of worshiping multiple gods. In some cases, mortal men were worshipped as gods. So is the case with Tammuz and his mother Ishtar, the two who the ancient Easter holiday was formed around. That ancient Roman celebration was used to shape our current Resurrection (Easter) celebration. Many also viewed the Emperor as God's man on Earth. These influences, and others, made it difficult for Roman Christians to understand monotheism and the true nature of Jesus. As the Son of God (the scriptural description), was He a man God? Was He just God's man on Earth? Maybe He was a combination somewhere between the two.

Only those high up in the church had copies of scripture to actually read. Even they could not agree on what they were reading. Two theologians, Arius and Athanasius from Alexandria, were well known throughout the empire for their differences of opinion on the subject. As they voiced their personal explanations of the nature of Jesus, divisions within the empire started to become evident. Historians have named their debate the Arian Controversy. Arius said it was the will of the Father that the Son came into being. The Father and Son were not of the same essence. Athanasius concluded that the divine nature in Jesus was identical to that of the Father and that Father and Son have the same substance. Their disagreement became a very public debate that pulled Roman citizens in different directions.

The Emperor Constantine felt political pressure as the Roman citizens chose sides in the controversy. After all, it was he who named Christianity as the official religion of the empire. He should be able to give the answers the people were seeking. He had to do something to hold the empire together. His solution, decide on an official description of who Jesus is. Once the Emperor made an official declaration on a religious issue the Roman citizens would accept it and follow. The hurdle he faced was he himself was not a well learned Christian. After all, he was a relatively new convert. To get around that small problem Constantine called together a council of those who were considered the leaders of the Christian religion within the empire. Athanasius and Arius were among the group.

Constantine's goal was to have the Council of Nicaea settle the controversy once and for all. His primary motive was to reunite the empire by eliminating the religious divide. Unfortunately, within the council the debate continued. Half of the attendees followed Athanasius and believed Jesus to be God. They relied mostly on confusing logic, supported by very little scripture. The other half followed Arius and believed Jesus to be the "begotten" Son of God, our divine Savior. The former group had the support of Roman religious tradition. The latter group had the support of scripture, but without a full understanding.

Constantine used the power of his position to settle the issue in a compromising manner. He said God and Jesus were homoousia. That is a Greek term which means "of the same substance." That allowed those who wanted to see Jesus as God to interpret this idea to mean that He was God. Those who wanted to see Jesus as begotten from God could interpret this to mean that he was born of God. Therefore, He shared many of the same likenesses of God but was not God Himself.

While this did not truly settle the debate, (it would continue for another century) it did supply enough for the council to draft a creed which, in part, says Jesus is:

> ... one Lord Jesus Christ,
> the only begotten Son of God,
> begotten of the Father,
> Light of light,
> Very God of very God,
> begotten not made,
> being of one substance with the Father...

Church leaders now had license to call Jesus God. Although the full cred begins by saying "We believe in one God," the phrases "Light of Light" and "very God from very God" would seem to indicate there are now two Gods. The use of the term "begotten" gives Jesus, the Son, His own identity, separate from God. But the creed quickly follows with "being of one substance." By this everyone is satisfied despite the contradictory statements. It was then officially acceptable to call both the Father "God" and the Son "God." The influence of Roman religious traditions carried more weight than scripture. Constantine achieved his goal. Both the Roman citizens who wanted to hold on to the tradition of polytheism and those who believed in monotheism seemed to be more closely united in one religion. The space between the two sides was not totally sealed, but a lot less noticeable.

Even though the original creed did not directly say so, the Holy Spirit would also be called God. Polytheists had the practice of grouping gods in threes because three was considered a perfect number. The term trinity had been actually used in pagan religions before Constantine accepted Christianity. Including the Holy Spirit in the one God satisfied that tradition. So, almost immediately they began saying "God the Father, God the Son, God the Holy Spirit." They then had the Christian "Trinity" (three). Yet, the theology of monotheism is maintained by saying the three persons exists all within one God. An important point to note: There were no scriptural references used to draw up the creed. Scriptural references were chosen later to justify the decision that was made and the teaching of the same. One often used scriptural reference was actually created and inserted into scripture. That will be discussed in detail in the next chapter.

The Nicaean council and its creed only made the declaration that Jesus was the second person of God. So, officially there were only two Gods in one. However, the concept of the trinity was a part of pagan religious tradition, including Roman religions, for several centuries before the council met. {Roman trinity: Jupiter, Maia, Mercury; Egyptian trinity: Amon, Ra, Ptah; Greek trinity: Zeus, Maia, Hermes; Babylonian trinity: Enki, Tammuz, Ishtar;

(Tammuz and Ishtar were adopted by the Romans and were the catalyst for the Easter holiday); and others.} That is why the use of the term trinity began almost immediately even though the third god, or third person of God, had not been officially identified.

Some of the Emperors that followed Constantine did not necessarily hold to the decisions made by the council and statements made in the creed. The Arion Controversy seemed to continue and re-ignite years after the council thought they had decided the issue.

The Emperor Theodosius I, who came into power in 379, was a strong supporter of the Nicaean Council's decision and its creed. However, he felt there was still a religious divide in the empire that needed to be addressed. In an effort to settle the controversy once and for all, he called for another council. The Council at Constantinople was convened in 381. The primary accomplishment of this council was the clear establishment of the Trinity Doctrine within the Roman Catholic Church. The wording of the existing creed was augmented to identify the Holy Spirit as the third person of God. The two creeds below show the changes that were made to serve that purpose.

**Original (Nicaean) Creed**

We believe in one God, the father almighty, Maker of heaven and earth, and of all things visible and invisible.

And in one Lord Jesus Christ, the only begotten Son of God, begotten of the Father, Light of light, Very God of very God, begotten not made, being of one substance with the Father; by whom all things were made; who for us men, and for our salvation, came down from heaven, and was incarnate and was made man; He suffered, and the third day he rose again, ascended into heaven, from there He shall come to judge both the quick and the dead; and in the Holy Spirit.

## New Creed (additions/changes in bold)

We believe in one God, the father almighty, Maker of heaven and earth, and of all things visible and invisible.

And in one Lord Jesus Christ, the only begotten Son of God, begotten of the Father *before all worlds,* light from light, Very God of very God, begotten not made, being of one substance with the Father; by whom all things were made;

who for us men, and for our salvation, came down *from heaven,* and *was incarnate **by the Holy Spirit of the Virgin Mary,** and* was made man; He ***was crucified for us under Pontius Pilate; and*** suffered ***and was buried;*** and the third day he rose again, ***according to the Scriptures, and*** ascended into heaven, ***and sitteth at the right hand of the Father; and he shall*** come ***again, with glory,*** to judge both the quick and the dead; **whose kingdom shall have no end.**

*And in the Holy Spirit,* ***the Lord, the Giver of Life; who proceedeth from the Father and the Son; who with the Father and the Son together is worshiped and glorified; who spake by the Prophets.*** *And Holy Catholic and Apostolic Church. I acknowledge one Baptism for the remission of sins; and I look for the resurrection of the dead, and the life of the world to come.* **Amen**

The original creed only states a belief in the Holy Spirit. The new creed makes a statement of His deity by saying He came from the Father and Son and are worshipped with the Father and Son. No scripture has ever been quoted that shows where the Holy Spirit came from. Such a statement is not in the Bible. This was simply a statement that was agreed upon by the group to justify continued use of the term Trinity when referring to God. A pagan tradition was now justified in the new religion. The Trinity was now an official Doctrine of the Roman Catholic Church. By placing the name Roman as the lead adjective in the name of the church, the empire claimed ownership of the religion. Therefore, from their perspective, the Trinity was an official doctrine of the Christian Religion.

# How is Scripture Applied?

The concept of the Trinity is called by the description "Doctrine." The use of that term was the subliminal way to instruct the Roman Christians to accept the teaching as the truth. However, any concept in the Christian religion that is called a doctrine should be taken from scripture, not just supported by chosen verses from scripture. That is where the teaching of the Trinity falls short. The concept of the trinity was decided upon to compromise a theological dispute. Scripture was applied only after the compromise was reached. Particular verses were chosen to justify the teaching. What is interesting is most resources on the subject use the same applied scripture verses. It is like reading a universal teacher's manual on teaching the Trinity. We will read a lot of scripture and discuss how they are used to teach the concept. We will also discuss how they are actually written and how they should be understood, in context, for reproof and correction.

As we read and study the scripture that are used to support the Trinity teaching, we will use as headings the four topics that are primarily used to teach the concept: There is only One God; One God Consists of Three Persons (Trinity); The Three Persons of God are distinguished one from another; Each Member of the Trinity is God. In some instances, other verses may be included in order to make sure we are reading their chosen verses in context to get the true and complete intended message. It is important to remember the concept of the Trinity was inserted into the Christian religion as the result of an initial effort to decide who Jesus is. Therefore, we will also address Who Does God Say Jesus Is and Who Does Jesus Say He Is. Those cannot be ignored because we know, "All scripture is given by inspiration of God..." (2 Timothy 3:16)

**There is Only One God**

This would seem to be the easiest topic to discuss. Both sides of the argument agree on this point. The basic premise of Christianity is monotheism, one God. The teaching of the Trinity begins also with the declaration there is only one God. The fact God had the wisdom to inspire men to write things down made it impossible to change that one truth. However, man found a way to manipulate that truth. Remember, again, the question that was being addressed when the Trinity was adopted was, "Who is Jesus?" Therefore, because the pagans were used to worshipping "gods," Jesus had to be made a part of the one God. That made it necessary to apply and explain some scripture in very creative ways. How can we have both the singular and the plural without changing what is written? Let us take a look.

***One God - Trinity teaching verses***

*Deuteronomy 6:4 – Hear, O Israel: The LORD our God is one LORD.*

*1 Corinthians 8:4 – ... and that there is none other God but one*

*Galatians 3:20 – Now a mediator is not a mediator of one, but God is one*

*James 2:19 – Thou believest that there is one God; thou doest well: the devils also believe, and tremble*

*The Concept of the Trinity Is Not Biblical*

*Isaiah 44:6 – Thus saith the LORD the King of Israel, and his redeemer the LORD of hosts; I am the first, and I am the last; and beside me there is no God*

*1 Kings 8:60 – That all the people of the earth may know that the LORD is God, and that there is none else*

*Isaiah 46:9 – For I am God, and there is none else; I am God, and there is none like me.*

There is no dispute about any of these verses. They all only mention God as the one. No other name is mentioned. There is no special explanation needed for these verses no matter which side of the argument you are on. God is the only God. The following verses, however, required some creative explanation. They are also used in Trinity teaching to express there is one God. How can you take God inspired scripture that puts God and Jesus in separate roles and turn around and say they are both one in the same? In Trinity teaching, while reading to find evidence of one God the remainder of each verse is to be ignored.

*1 Timothy 2:5 – For there is one God, and one mediator between God and men, the man Christ Jesus;*

*1 Corinthians 8:6 – But to us there is but one God, the Father, of whom are all things, and we in him; and one LORD Jesus Christ, by whom are all things, and we by him.*

*Mark 12:29 – [29]And Jesus answered him, The first of all the commandments is, Hear, O Israel; The LORD our God is one LORD:*

*John 17:3 – And this is life eternal, that they might know thee the only true God, and Jesus Christ, whom thou hast sent*

The verse from 1 Timothy describes Jesus as the "...mediator between God and men...." Again, it is obvious Jesus is being shown to be separate from the one God. God is not His own mediator. This is one of the areas that Trinity teaching says God manifests Himself in three distinct persons. While Jesus is shown as being separate, it is taught He is still fully God. Galatians 3:20 could have been added to this group. It says, "... a mediator is not a mediator of one...." God inspired both verses to be written. He would not have contradicted Himself to be His own mediator. The use of the word "and" also indicates separation between God and the mediator, the man Christ Jesus.

The verse from 1 Corinthians begins with the phrase, "But to us...." That signifies we, as mortals, should recognize God and Jesus as they are described therein. God is the Father. Jesus holds the position over us as Lord. Some will say the title Lord identifies Jesus as God. That is how the verse is applied in Trinity teaching. The truth is the title Lord sometimes refers to God the Father and sometimes to Jesus the Son. It depends on who, in a given passage, is being described as the one in authority. Lord is also used in scripture to describe a Kings authority over his people. Would a king who lords over his people be a god? This verse describes Jesus as the one who has authority over us (But to us...). That authority was given to Hm by God the Father. (Mathew 11:27, 28:18) He did not give it to himself. Therefore, they are not one in the same. Again, it says here there is one God "and" one Lord. More importantly for this discussion we are told here the one God is the Father. That leaves no room to call the Son or the Holy Spirit God. To say otherwise is to contradict God who inspired the scripture to be written.

The verse from Mark is Jesus speaking to a scribe before His death and resurrection. He had not yet been given all authority that is why He called God the "One Lord." He was not referring to Himself. In fact, He was including Himself in the group of "our" when He said "our God." God is even Jesus's Lord. Jesus is not His own Lord. This is yet another instance where Trinity teachers will say Jesus is distinctly separate from God but still God. They repeat that statement without showing scripture that makes such a statement That is one of those creative explanations mentioned earlier. This verse definitely shows Jesus is separate from God. It also shows He does not consider Himself to be God.

John tells us Jesus was sent by "the only true God." There is God "and" Jesus. Because the verse describes God and His Son Separately, we cannot decide among ourselves to read the verse as, "the only true God and God Jesus." God sent His Son not Himself.

Theses verses are sometimes used in the teaching that there is only One God. That is a true statement that can be taken from these and many other verses in scripture. But, again, who Is Jesus is the question they were attempting to answer when the doctrine of the Trinity was added to Christianity. That is why it was necessary to be creative and say Jesus is both separate from, and still a part of, God. You are first taught the concept then expected to read it into the verses. They could not allow these verses to show (reproof) their decision and creed were incorrect.

### *One God Consists of Three Persons*

Once the adopters of the Trinity doctrine felt comfortable with their descriptions of the one God, they then had to show the One was really multiple. First, they declared two; then, while applying a pagan tradition, three. That is the primary concept that must be believed to even make the claim there is a Trinity. The use of the term trinity means three-in-one. There are several verses in scripture that are used to describe the multiple Gods they want. First, the concept of the Trinity is taught. Then verses are chosen to support or justify the teaching. In some cases, creative translating was the tool used to support the teaching. Do any of the verses directly describe three-in-one? That is what must be shown to truly justify the teaching of the Trinity as doctrine.

As stated in the preface, The King James Version (KJV) is the translation that will be used for scripture quotations for consistency purposes. However, there is a reason it is the English translation used most often to teach the doctrine. With that being said, there are two verses whose translation in the KJV is very different from other English language translations. When discussing or teaching the Trinity, 1 John 5:7-8 are often the first verses quoted. They are always quoted, in English, exclusively from the KJV or its variations. Verse 7, in particular, seems to teach the very heading above. That single verse makes the foundation statement for the doctrine. However, Bible scholars overwhelmingly agree the KJV translation of these two verses does not reflect the God inspired words of the original writer (John). So, what do the verses say? Let's read them in various English translations.

- KJV – [7]For there are three that bear record in heaven, the Father, the Word, and the Holy Ghost: and these three are one. [8]And there are three that bear witness in earth, the Spirit, and the water, and the blood: and these three agree in one
- NIV – [7]For there are three that testify: [8]the Spirit, the water, and the blood; and the three are in agreement.
- NASB – [7]For there are three that testify: [8] the Spirit and the water and the blood; and the three are in agreement.
- NLT – [7]So we have these three witnesses[a]— [8] the Spirit, the water, and the blood—and all three agree.
- ESV – [7]And it is the Spirit that beareth witness, because the Spirit is the truth. [8]For there are three who bear witness, the Spirit, and the water, and the blood: and the three agree in one

## The Concept of the Trinity Is Not Biblical

It is pretty obvious, of the five translations shown here, the KJV stands alone as one proclaiming the Trinity in verse 7. That should not be. As different translations are written minor differences in wording can be expected. That would be due to the accuracy of the various translators' knowledge and ability to interpret the original language. But, having a totally different message is not acceptable. Why is the KJV so different from the others?

History shows the wording of these two verses, as we find them in the KJV, was not found in any translation of the Bible, Greek or English, until the sixteenth century. The text was found, however, in the Latin Vulgate which was the text used by the "Roman" Catholic Church. Remember, it was a Roman council that initiated the creed calling Jesus God. A few years later the Holy Spirit was added by another council and the use of the title Trinity was justified. While the translation of the New Testament (NT) from Greek to Latin (Vulgate) was taking place, some revisions were made to better support Roman Catholic teaching. Those revisions included the addition of the verses in question.

The Roman Empire was in existence until the mid-1400s. That longevity allowed the influence of the Catholic Church to spread throughout Europe. Services in the Catholic Church, even outside of Latin speaking countries, were conducted in Latin. The Trinity was a foundational part of Catholic teaching. The Protestant Reformation (1517–1555) had not yet happened. Therefore, many of the Roman Catholic Teachings and practices had taken a stronghold within the Christian religion. Even after the reformation some of their doctrine and practices remained.

In 1516 a new Greek translation of the NT, written by one named Erasmus, was released. Catholic Church leaders raised a ruckus because it did not contain the wording in the verses from 1 John that would establish the Trinity (known as the Comma Johanneum). Erasmus explained he did not include that wording because there were no Greek references to it in any form. Indeed, prior to this the only mention of the Comma Johanneum, in Greek, was in a Latin work called the Acts of the Lateran Council that had been translated into Greek only a year earlier. A second edition of Erasmus' NT, released a couple of years later, also did not contain the wording the Catholic Church wanted. Again, there were no original Greek manuscripts of any kind that contained the Comma. To overcome this hurdle, the Catholic Church had a manuscript produced in Greek that contained the wording. In 1520 a Franciscan Friar named Roy (or Froy), at Oxford, took the words from the Latin Vulgate and included them in a manuscript he wrote in the Greek language. That document was made known to Erasmus. Now that he was aware a manuscript existed that was written in Greek originally, and contained the Comma, he gave in to the pressure from the Catholic Church. The Comma Johanneum was included in his third edition of the NT in 1522.

When King James commissioned his translation in 1604 (released in 1611) he instructed the NT translators to use only Greek text. He did not want them to be influenced by any current English or Latin (Catholic) versions of the Bible. As a result of the reformation there were many translations with noticeable differences. His desire was to circumvent those differences. Unfortunately the third edition of the Erasmus version of the Greek NT was the one used. Was it chosen deliberately to maintain the doctrine of the Trinity they may have already been taught and believed? After all, the doctrine had been created almost thirteen centuries before the KJV was written. It had saturated the Christian religion throughout Europe. Maybe it was just a lack of knowledge there were differences in Greek translations also. These were the same types of differences King James wanted to avoid in English translations. This new Greek translation was less than 100 years old. Was that enough time, in those days, for controversies to be voiced abroad? We may never know for sure.

An important note: The reason Erasmus initially refused to include the Comma Johanneum in his first two editions was for accuracy. He wanted to make sure his version of the NT could be verified by any and all means available in existing Greek manuscripts. That is important to know for those who use the KJV as their primary source of God's Word. Other than the verses we have been discussing here (1 John 5:7–8) (and a few other small errors and additions) the KJV is still, foe the most part, a reliable translation of the Holy Bible and can be trusted. The addition of these two verses, manipulated by the Roman Catholic Church, does not nullify the remainder of Erasmus' meticulous efforts. Fortunately, the majority of the Erasmus Greek version remained unchanged. Some of the other small errors, that may have been made by the KJV translators, can be attributed to the influence of prior Catholic teaching. The same would be true for any translation. When reading the KJV and other translations we should follow the advice of 2 Timothy 2:15. Study to shew thyself approved unto God, a workman that needeth not to be ashamed, rightly dividing the word of truth.

The two verses in question were examined in a total of 62 English language Bible translations. The wording of the Comma Johanneum was found in only 17 (27%) of them. Four of that group were direct variations of the KJV. That is enough of a discrepancy to say with confidence the wording, intended to establish the Trinity, is not a part of the original God inspired text.

Recap: The epistle of 1 John was written in the first century. Both the Nicene Council and the Council of Constantinople were convened in the fourth century. The Roman Empire (Catholic Church) instilled the pagan doctrine of the Trinity into the Christian religion. To justify the doctrine, the Comma Johanneum was added to the Latin translation of the Bible (the Vulgate) as it was translated from the Greek NT. After several centuries it was manipulated and pressured to be included in a Greek version of the NT. Then, either by ignorance or choice, it made its way into an English translation (KJV). The bottom line is 1 John 5:7–8, as written in the KJV, is a Roman Catholic Church insertion into the Bible, not God inspired scripture. Your trust in the teaching of the Trinity should not be based on 1 John 5:7 alone. There must be other scriptural proofs.

Following are several other verses of scripture that are used to teach One God Consists of Three Persons. Let us take a look.

These are but a few of the verses that are commonly quoted to support the statement that the Trinity consists of three persons in one God. Before discussing the individual verses, it is important to understand two concepts that come into play while reading. The first is having the ability to interpret what a text is saying without the influence of prior knowledge or expectations. That is called exegesis; taking or gaining knowledge from the text. The second concept is having prior knowledge or expectations for what a text will say and reading the text to find support for what one thinks they already know. That is called eisegesis; reading information into the text. When the given verses are read objectively it will become obvious eisegesis is the only way the Trinity can be found therein. As said before, the concept was first taught then the verses chosen.

*Genesis 1:26 – And God said, Let us make man in our image, after our likeness...*

*3:22 – And the LORD God said, Behold, the man is become as one of us...*

*11:7 – Go to, let us go down, and there confound their language...*

*Isaiah 6:8 – Also I heard the voice of the LORD, saying, Whom shall I send, and who will go for us? Then said I, Here am I; send me*

All three verses from Genesis, along with Isaiah 6:8, uses the plural pronoun "us." A person looking for the Trinity will automatically read the "us" as describing three persons. In truth there is no specific numerical value attached to the word "us." It does tell us, however, there was more than one entity present as God spoke the words. There is no indication God was talking to Himself or a different part of Himself. When the verses are read exegetically there is no way to attach the number three. God is speaking. But there is nothing that says He is referring to Himself in the plural. If you do believe He was talking to Himself in plural, then you must answer another question. Was He talking to only one of His other selves or both of His other selves? How many other selves exist?

God is spirit. (John 4:24) He is not the only entity, however, that exists in the spirit realm. (Zechariah 6:5, Revelation 1:4) In fact, God had sons in the heavenly realm. (Job 1:6) So, the word "us" will only be limited to the number three if you were first taught that to be its meaning.

*Isaiah 48:16 – [16]Come ye near unto me, hear ye this; I have not spoken in secret from the beginning; from the time that it was, there am I: and now the LORD God, and his Spirit, hath sent me*

The phrase "… the Lord God and His Spirit …" in the above verse is also taught to represent two-in-one. Any time God and a spirit are mentioned in the same passage Trinity teachers would have you to believe so. You are to believe it can only be the one we refer to as the Holy Spirit. Referring again to Revelation, the same seven spirits that are "before His throne" in 1:4 are called spirits of God in 3:1 and other verses. Are you prepared to say God is seven-in-one? Before claims of a trinity or any other multiple is associated with God, it must be shown He is the only one who exists in His form and on the spiritual realm. The Bible, God's inspired Word, does not teach that.

*Matthew 3:16–17 And Jesus, when he was baptized, went up straightway out of the water: and, lo, the heavens were opened unto him, and he saw the Spirit of God descending like a dove, and lighting upon him: [17]And lo a voice from heaven, saying, This is my beloved Son, in whom I am well pleased.*

*28:19 Go ye therefore, and teach all nations, baptizing them in the name of the Father, and of the Son, and of the Holy Ghost:*

The verses from Matthew show even more clearly the separation of the three persons. Trinity teachers hope their teaching will cause you to read into the verses that the three individuals represent the one God. In verses 3:16 Jesus is on Earth having just been baptized. The Spirit, alone, descends from Heaven. God is still in Heaven. The most important parts of these verses are God's own words (vs. 17). He did not describe Jesus as a part of Himself. He, God, said Jesus is His Son. The only way to see them as parts of one is if that is what you wanted them to be when you read the passage. The Nicaean Creed was the first document to make such a claim. At the time of its creation there were no scripture references showing from where the concept was taken. God does not say here, or anywhere else, this is a part of me in who I am well pleased.

We have already read verses where God is described as the Father. In verse 28:19 the title "God" does not appear in front of the Son or the Holy Ghost. Only if reading with eisegesis would one insert words that do not exist. We are baptized in the name of the Father and the Son and the Holy Spirit because all three play important individual roles in our spiritual lives.

*2 Corinthians 13:14 – The grace of the LORD Jesus Christ, and the love of God, and the communion of the Holy Ghost, be with you all. Amen.*

Each time the Father (God) the Son (Jesus) and the Holy Spirit are mentioned in the same passage we are expected to believe they represent the one God. If that were the case there would be no need for the above verse to name all three. The verse shows three separate persons serving us in three different ways. Nothing there says the three are one. If God wanted us to recognize a Trinity, He would have made it plain. Instead, he said, "But to us..." (1Corinthians 8:6).

Unless you read into these, or any other verses of scripture, there are three-in-one you will not find it. (1 John 5:7–8 has already been discussed.) Without any scripture verses that actually say the one God manifests Himself in three persons there is no Trinity as it is taught. Despite that fact, we will look at a few verses under the next subtitle because the stated topic is essential to Trinity teaching.

***Three Persons of God are distinguished one from another.***

The verses in this section are also quoted on both sides of the debate. The difference is how they are applied by the teachers on either side. One side applies the verses literally. The other side applies the verses to justify a certain teaching. The previous section suggests the latter application. The difficulty in applying these verses to Trinity teaching is obvious. The topic is not relevant unless prior teaching of scripture has shown that God does manifest Himself as three persons. More importantly, you will have had to accept the Trinity teaching. If you read scripture objectively (exegesis) you know God is not shown to be three. Only reading with the influence of Trinity teaching (eisegesis) will you see God as three. In fact, scripture tells us this particular topic is how we should see the Father, Son, and Holy Spirit; as individuals. The verses we will discuss here would seem to be further confirmation that the Trinity is not a true biblical concept. Never-the-less, we will take a look because this topic is used to tie the previous and following topics together in Trinity teaching. One quick observation: The Trinity concept was adopted while attempting to determine who Jesus is. Jesus is a New Testament Figure. Yes, He did fulfill Old Testament prophesies. Still, one must ask why is so much Old Testament (OT) used in the justification efforts?

*Genesis 19:24 – Then the LORD rained upon Sodom and upon Gomorrah brimstone and fire from the LORD out of heaven;*

*Hosea 1:4 – And the LORD said unto him, Call his name Jezreel; for yet a little while, and I will avenge the blood of Jezreel upon the house of Jehu, and will cause to cease the kingdom of the house of Israel.*

These two verses are often prefaced with a statement that tries to show a distinction between LORD and Lord. In their attempt they spell the first LORD with all uppercase letters and the second Lord with only the lead letter being upper case. In the verse from Hosea the name Lord only appears once. When these verses are read in context, it is obvious all three uses of the name Lord refer to God speaking. Why they think changing the letter case creates two different Lords is a mystery. The KJV uses all uppercase letters in all three uses of the name. Although it does not show here, we must remember even the KJV was translated many years after the Trinity doctrine was initiated. The translators may have been influenced in some manner.

*Psalm 2:7 – I will declare the decree: the LORD hath said unto me, Thou art my Son; this day have I begotten thee*

*2:11–12 – Serve the* LORD *with fear, and rejoice with trembling. Kiss the Son, lest he be angry, and ye perish from the way, when his wrath is kindled but a little. Blessed are all they that put their trust in him*

*Proverbs 30:4 Who hath ascended up into heaven, or descended? who hath gathered the wind in his fists? who hath bound the waters in a garment? who hath established all the ends of the earth? what is his name, and what is his son's name, if thou canst tell?*

These verses are quoted to establish the fact God has a son. That is another fact that is not in dispute. That is the very distinction that is given to Jesus. God called Jesus His Son. We also know many OT verses prophetically told of Jesus's coming. With Psalms and Proverbs being books of worship and wisdom, these verses should be read in that vein. The Bible actually tells us God had more than one son. (Job 1:6, 2:1, 38:7) Jesus is the only "begotten" Son. (John 3:16) This is where Jesus was discussed while he was still in the same form as God. (Philippians 2:6) While in the flesh He did fulfill these and other prophesies.

*Numbers 27:18 And the* LORD *said unto Moses, Take thee Joshua the son of Nun, a man in whom is the spirit, and lay thine hand upon him;*

*Psalm 51:10–12 Create in me a clean heart, O God; and renew a right spirit within me. Cast me not away from thy presence; and take not thy holy spirit from me. Restore unto me the joy of thy salvation; and uphold me with thy free spirit.*

First let's agree the "Lord" in the Numbers verse and "God" in the Psalms verse are the same one God. Many verses throughout the Bible could have been used to show the distinction between God and the Holy Spirit. Why these verses are often used in Trinity teaching is questionable. Is there a covert attempt to create a distinction between God and this use of the name Lord? Again, the fact that God is distinctly different from the Holy Spirt, and the two of them from Jesus, is the very proof (reproof) that the Trinity is not a Biblical concept. Of course, the distinction will not be so obvious to anyone who has accepted the Trinity teaching.

There is no indication the spirit in Joshua was God. It is true the Lord and that spirit are distinct individuals. In this case having "the spirit" could mean having a righteous attitude. When a person has a true desire to serve God and do His will, he/she has the right spirit. Of course, if you have that right attitude, it is because of the influence of the Holy Spirit. The writer of the Psalms verse did not want to lose that spiritual influence and guidance. This verse actually says, "renew a right spirit within me." It would seem that particular phrase is referring to a righteous attitude. We may at time lose the desire to serve. Here he is asking God to restore that desire in him. Again, we can agree God and the Holy Spirit are separate and distinct individuals.

*Psalm 45:6–7 Thy throne, O God, is for ever and ever: the sceptre of thy kingdom is a right sceptre. Thou lovest righteousness, and hatest wickedness: therefore God, thy God, hath anointed thee with the oil of gladness above thy fellows.*

*Hebrews 1:8–9 But unto the Son he saith, Thy throne, O God, is for ever and ever: a sceptre of righteousness is the sceptre of thy kingdom. Thou hast loved righteousness, and hated iniquity; therefore God, even thy God, hath anointed thee with the oil of gladness above thy fellows.*

These two sets of verses are quoted for the purpose of showing a distinction between God the Father and God the Son. When reading the Hebrews verses, as they are presented, it does appear the Son is being called God. Obviously, the verses from Hebrews are an NT teaching of OT scripture. The writer of Hebrews is following Jesus's instructions (Matthew 28:20). Jesus said to teach all things He commanded. Jesus taught from the scriptures we call the Old Testament. That is what the writer was doing here. Therefore, we must first study the verses as written in Psalms. This is a case where the verses absolutely must be read in context. We will read book 45 of Psalms beginning at verse one and continuing through verse eight.

*My heart is inditing a good matter: I speak of the things which I have made touching the king: my tongue is the pen of a ready writer. ² Thou art fairer than the children of men: grace is poured into thy lips: therefore God hath blessed thee forever.³ Gird thy sword upon thy thigh, O most mighty, with thy glory and thy majesty.*

*⁴ And in thy majesty ride prosperously because of truth and meekness and righteousness; and thy right hand shall teach thee terrible things. ⁵ Thine arrows are sharp in the heart of the king's enemies; whereby the people fall under thee. ⁶ Thy throne, O God, is for ever and ever: the sceptre of thy kingdom is a right sceptre.*

*⁷ Thou lovest righteousness, and hatest wickedness: therefore God, thy God, hath anointed thee with the oil of gladness above thy fellows. ⁸ All thy garments smell of myrrh, and aloes, and cassia, out of the ivory palaces, whereby they have made thee glad.*

The psalmist is writing about some good things concerning the King (vs. 1) The King has been blessed by God because he is very fair and shows grace to the people(vs.2). Because he demonstrates truth, meekness, and righteousness he can ride majestically and will be prosperous (vs. 2,3) He will also show success against his enemies (vs. 5). Verses 3, 4, and 5 are stating how the king can carry himself and what he can expect because of the blessings he received from God in verse 2. Now in verse 6 the writer is actually speaking directly to God. He is saying God will rule forever and his ruling and authority are right. Would you say, based on verse 6, the King is God? I think not. In verses 7 the attention is turned back to the king. Because he has the preciously stated qualities God, his God, has anointed him. Verse8 tells of some of the things the king has been blessed with that makes him glad.

It is important that the chosen verses (6 and 7) be read in context to get the full and true meaning. It is too easy to cherry pick a couple of verses and apply to them the meaning you want them to have. Even Satan did that when he tried to tempt Jesus to jump off of the temple (Matthew 4:6). This passage in Psalms is talking about the King (vs. 1), not the Son of God. Therefore, it is more reproof the title God the Son is definitely incorrect.

Now let's examine the chosen verses (1:8–9) from Hebrews. Remember, first, the OT passage came before the NT passage. The writer of Hebrews was re-teaching or re-applying the passage from Psalms (as instructed in the Great Commission). The purpose of this passage is to show how highly esteemed Jesus is in God's eyes. That is how we should see Jesus when looking from the proper perspective. To get the whole picture we will begin reading at verse one and continue through verse 10.

*The Concept of the Trinity Is Not Biblical*

*¹God, who at sundry times and in divers manners spake in time past unto the fathers by the prophets, ²Hath in these last days spoken unto us by his Son, whom he hath appointed heir of all things, by whom also he made the worlds; ³Who being the brightness of his glory, and the express image of his person, and upholding all things by the word of his power, when he had by himself purged our sins, sat down on the right hand of the Majesty on high: ⁴Being made so much better than the angels, as he hath by inheritance obtained a more excellent name than they. ⁵For unto which of the angels said he at any time, Thou art my Son, this day have I begotten thee? And again, I will be to him a Father, and he shall be to me a Son? ⁶ And again, when he bringeth in the firstbegotten into the world, he saith, And let all the angels of God worship him. ⁷And of the angels he saith, Who maketh his angels spirits, and his ministers a flame of fire. ⁸But unto the Son he saith, Thy throne, O God, is for ever and ever: a sceptre of righteousness is the sceptre of thy kingdom. ⁹Thou hast loved righteousness, and hated iniquity; therefore God, even thy God, hath anointed thee with the oil of gladness above thy fellows. ¹⁰And, Thou, LORD, in the beginning hast laid the foundation of the earth; and the heavens are the works of thine hands:*

Again, the chosen verses (8 and 9) are intended to establish Jesus as God the Son. The writer begins by identifying God and how He communicates to us Vs. (1–2a). The second half of verse 2 shows God and His Son are not the same entity. God "appointed" His Son heir of all. One cannot be heir of his own. The description of the Son continues in verses 3 and 4. Verse 3 states three important points for this discussion. The Son is the "express image" of God. Being the image of God says the Son is not God. Otherwise, we could claim to be gods. (Genesis 1:26) One cannot be the image of himself.

The Son (Jesus) purged our sins. He died on the cross, not God. The Son then "sat down on the right hand of the Majesty on high." The Son sat down next to God. He did not go back to be God or a part of God. Jesus's name is above all others by inheritance (vs. 4) not by being the second part of three-in-one. Verse 5 clearly tells us God makes the distinction between Himself, the Father, and Jesus, the Son. One cannot be both/either a father to himself and/or a son to himself. The Father and Son are not one. Again, it is God who is in charge in verses 6 and 7, having His angels worship the Son.

It is critical that an understanding of verses 1 through 7 was discussed before reading the chosen verses (8 and 9). They show God and the Son are individuals and God is the one making the decisions. The Son is the begotten one (vs. 5 and 6) who received His position by inheritance (vs. 4). God has always been the one in charge.

Verse 8 begins with "But unto the Son he saith." Then the quote of Psalm 45 begins. Because we are first taught the concept of God the Son, this verse seems to call the Son God. That is why it was so important to read the passage in Psalms 45 first. Just as the psalmist wrote verse 6 (8b in Hebrews) to praise God, the writer of Hebrews paused here to do the same. The writer showed, in the previous verses, that God established the Son over the angels. He took this moment to say God is in charge and His decisions and authority are right. He resumed his statement to the Son with verse 9 just as the psalmist did to the king in his verse 7. When speaking to the Son in verse 9 the writer referred to God as His (the Son's) God. That statement also shows the Son is not God. Could the Son be His own God?

A lot of time has been spent discussing the chosen verses from Psalm 45 and its quote from Hebrews 1. This was necessary to make sure the verses were read from the proper perspective. If someone read only the chosen verses in Hebrews, they would definitely come to the conclusion that the Son is God. Too often we read only the verses that our teacher asks us to read. Without knowing many NT passages are quotes from the OT our understanding is limited to the teacher's perspective. In this case, knowing the context of the verses in the OT allows us to better understand how they were applied when quoted in the NT. The Father said the Son is His Son. He also said He is a Father to Him. Why do we wish to say differently? The two of them are distinguished from each other because they are not two in one. We must study diligently if we are going to be able to rightly divide the word of truth.

## *Each Member of the Trinity is God*

This section absolutely must be coupled with the previous two sections to establish the Trinity. Although the scripture referred to previously has not shown God to exist in three persons, that claim can still be made if scripture allows both Jesus and the Holy Spirit to be God as well as the Father. Here each of the three persons will be discussed individually in an effort to show scripture can be used to described each as God. If they cannot all be individually described as God by scripture the doctrine of the Trinity cannot stand. The following verses must be read in context to be sure that both who is speaking, and who is being referred to, are/is God.

### *The Father is God.*

There is no dispute here. This is in the same category as the subtitle "There is Only One God." The question that comes into play is, is the Father only the first person of the One Triune God? These verses are used in all Trinity teaching because the Father is always the first one named in the description of the Trinity; God the Father, God the Son, God the Holy Spirit.

> *John 6:27 – Labour not for the meat which perisheth, but for that meat which endureth unto everlasting life, which the Son of man shall give unto you: for him hath God the Father sealed.*

*Romans 1:7 – To all that be in Rome, beloved of God, called to be saints: Grace to you and peace from God our Father, and the Lord Jesus Christ.*

*1 Peter 1:2 – Elect according to the foreknowledge of God the Father, through sanctification of the Spirit, unto obedience and sprinkling of the blood of Jesus Christ: Grace unto you, and peace, be multiplied.*

As stated, there is no dispute that the Father is God. It could be stated in the inverse. God is the Father. However, Trinity teaching will not allow the inverse to be a complete statement. These are not the only verses that make the statement God the Father. Other verses that could have been chosen are Matthew 11:27, Romans 15:6, 1 Corinthians 8:6, 2 Corinthians 1:3, and others.

Notice in the verse from John, God the Father sealed the Son. That indicates they were two separate persons. If the Son is God would there have been a need for one person of the Trinity to seal another person of the Trinity? Also note the verse does not say God the Son was sealed by God the Father. The term "and" in the Romans verse also shows God our Father "and" the Lord Jesus Christ are two persons. God is called Our Father while Jesus is called Lord and Christ. That shows the two separate functions in our lives by the two separate persons. God, the Spirit, and Jesus are serving three separate functions in the 1 Peter verse. Still, this verse only refers to the Father as God. Neither the Spirit nor Jesus is called God. Yes, the Father is God.

The sole purpose of this topic is to give the impression the Father is only one of the persons of God. They first teach there are three persons in the one God. Those who have accepted that teaching will read into these verses the Father is only the first person of God. That subjective view is taken because you already know the other two persons are going to be described as God also. The truth is, only the Father is God.

## The Holy Spirit is God

*Acts 5:3–4 – [3] But Peter said, Ananias, why hath Satan filled thine heart to lie to the Holy Ghost, and to keep back part of the price of the land? [4] Whiles it remained, was it not thine own? and after it was sold, was it not in thine own power? why hast thou conceived this thing in thine heart? thou hast not lied unto men, but unto God.*

*1 Corinthians 3:16 – Know ye not that ye are the temple of God, and that the Spirit of God dwelleth in you?*

This section is relatively short. The usual sources do not have many chosen verses to support the teaching that the Holy Spirit is God. The Holy Spirit was added by the Roman Catholic Church as a person of God because in Roman culture the number three was considered a perfect number. It was more acceptable to the polytheistic to have a God of three (Trinity) than a God of two. There were absolutely no scriptural references made when "who proceedeth from the Father and the Son" was added to the creed. The same is true of the addition of "who with the Father and the Son together is worshiped and glorified." The term trinity was already being used before the Council at Constantinople was convened. It was brought over from pagan religious traditions. The Emperor Theodosius I wanted to make it an official doctrine for the Roman Catholic Church. Saying the Holy Spirit is God is merely a commandment of men (Mark 7:7).

The two verses mentioned above are repeated several times in Trinity teaching sources. Neither of them actually makes the desired statement.

The verses from Acts are discussing Ananias' deceitful act. He is being informed that when he lied it was to God. All of our intentional acts of sin are against God. The Holy Spirit was sent to

Earth to do God's will. Scripture says He is not working for Himself. (John 16:13) That is why when we lie to Him we are really lying to God. Analogy: Your father sends you to the market to pick up a certain quantity of product he has already paid for. The store keeper holds back a portion of what is owed thinking to himself you do not have all of the numbers. You were not deciding for yourself how much to pick up. You were carrying out your father's wishes. The store keeper thinks he has only fooled you. He has really cheated your father. The fact you are the one who went to the market does not make you your father. Our acts may be in the sight of man but the sin is against God.

There are many verses in scripture that refer to the Spirit of God just as the chosen verse from 1 Corinthians does. We must know there are many entities in the Spirit realm who are doing the will of God the Father. Just as Jesus said He was not doing anything of himself, so is the same with the Holy Spirit. They are both only doing what they have been directed to do by God. Jesus is the Son of God and our Savior. The spirit that dwells in us to do God's will as our Comforter and Sprit of Truth would be described as the Spirit of God. The title alone does not make him to be the third person of God. Verses from Revelation that mentioned the seven spirits of God have already been mentioned. This is simply another case where the concept was first taught then verses were chosen to support the teaching. There is no verse in scripture that directly says either title, the Holy Spirit, the Holy Ghost, the Spirit of Truth, or the Spirit of God refers only to God. We do know the Spirit(s), called by either title, is doing the will of God not His own. But, He is not God.

*The Son is God.*

This title statement alone creates its own oxymoron. We have already shown the Father to be God. One cannot be both Father and Son. That statement is true in a logical, common-sense perspective.

It is especially true when the Son was begotten. Yet, verses have been chosen out of scripture to support the claim. We are taught to overlook that realistic impossibility by the statement, "how that can be true is a mystery only possible with God." This section, in fact, presents the strongest argument in favor of the Trinity.

Without intense study, the chosen verses do appear, to some degree, to refer to Jesus as God. Remember, initially only two were named God by the Nicaean Council and its creed; the Father and the Son. That was simply a decision made by men, not taken from scripture. Their purpose was to settle a disagreement about who Jesus is. The emperor needed Him to fit comfortably into traditional Roman religious culture to mend the religious/political divide happening within the empire. The support scripture verses were chosen after the decision was made. Several verses were augmented in the Latin translation to give support to the doctrine. The inclusion of the Holy spirit, and the official title Trinity, came later.

This section is lengthy. A lot of information is contained in this discussion that is needed to bring out the truth. Still, not every verse of scripture that is used to teach the Son is God will be covered. The most commonly used verses will be discussed in context and in detail. The correct understanding of scripture is vital. Let's begin.

*Isaiah 7:14 – Therefore the Lord himself shall give you a sign; Behold, a virgin shall conceive, and bear a son, and shall call his name Immanuel.*

*Matthew 1:22–23 – Now all this was done, that it might be fulfilled which was spoken of the Lord by the prophet, saying, [23] Behold, a virgin shall be with child, and shall bring forth a son, and they shall call his name Emmanuel, which being interpreted is, God with us.*

These two verses should be discussed within the same conversation. Isaiah 7:14 is most often quoted as being a prophetical statement. It is said to foretell of the virgin Mary giving birth to God in the person of Jesus. The quote from Matthew 1:23 is used as the proof statement. In the Catholic Church, Mary is called the Mother of God. Remembering the OT was written originally in Hebrew, the Isaiah verse should be translated from Hebrew not Greek.

Some may ask why the statement about translation needed to be said. Greek was one of the two major languages of the Roman Empire. The generation of Hebrew descendants (Jewish) who grew up under Roman rule spoke Greek as their primary language. That is the reason the NT was originally written in Greek. The transition to the Greek language took place hundreds of years before the birth of Jesus. The change in primary language brought on the need to translate the OT, written originally in Hebrew, into Greek. That is said to have taken place during the third century B.C. The Greek translation of the OT is commonly called the Septuagint. Many of the NT quotes were taken from the Septuagint. Many of the subsequent OT translations were also done from the Septuagint rather than from the Hebrew text.

When God led the Prophet Isaiah to record his book, it was written in the Hebrew language. That is the reason this particular verse should be studied in the original language. As the OT was translated into Greek there were some minor changes made that makes a major difference. We are taught this verse was quoted in Matthew 1:23 as fulfillment of a prophesy. When read from the Septuagint, as the Disciples did, it very well could be taken that way. However, the verse in Isaiah should be studied from the original language and in context.

The two key words, from the Septuagint and the Matthew quote, that must be studied are "virgin" and the name "Immanuel." The phrase "a virgin shall conceive" is used to declare the verse is a prophecy of the virgin Mary giving birth to Jesus. The most

## The Concept of the Trinity Is Not Biblical

common meaning that is given for the name Immanuel is "God with us." That is used to say, in the teaching of the Trinity, Jesus is God. In order to make that claim, the two names Immanuel and Jesus, are said to have the same meaning. We must look at the verse and its meanings in the original Hebrew.

The Hebrew word that is translated virgin in the Septuagint, and consequently, the KJV is "almah." The literal translation for "almah" is a "young woman." There is no connotation of sexuality in the word. The Hebrew word for virgin is "betulah." That word does not appear in this verse at all. It does appear elsewhere in Isaiah (23:4). That lets us know if 7:14 was intended to say virgin "betulah" would have been used. "Almah" is the word given to Isaiah by God to express the message He was giving. The error in translation is believed to have occurred with the creation of the Septuagint. We cannot be sure, but the Greek culture may have influenced the translators. Some modern translations use the proper term "young Woman" but adds phrases like, "who had not been with a man", to maintain the idea of a virgin. Those phrases are often in parenthesis to show they are not originally in scripture. Being influenced by erroneous teaching, they have changed the truth into a lie.

When translated directly from the Hebrew, the name Immanuel means "with us is the mighty one." Most translations use the phrase "God is with us." That slight difference is insignificant because most people will see the "mighty one" as being "God." What is significant for this discussion about the Trinity is whether the name means God will be with us in the flesh. That is the meaning and understanding that is taught from the Matthew 1:23 quote. The intention is to support the teaching that Jesus is God in the flesh. To see the true application of the meaning of the name, Isaiah should be read in context.

## Isaiah 7:10–16

| From Hebrew text | KJV |
|---|---|
| 10: And the L-RD spoke again unto Ahaz, saying: | [10] Moreover the LORD spake again unto Ahaz, saying, |
| 11: 'Ask thee a sign of the L-RD thy G-d: ask it either in the depth, or in the height above.' | [11] Ask thee a sign of the LORD thy God; ask it either in the depth, or in the height above. |
| 12: But Ahaz said: 'I will not ask, neither will I try the L-RD.' | [12] But Ahaz said, I will not ask, neither will I tempt the LORD. |
| 13: And he said: 'Hear ye now, O house of David: Is it a small thing for you to weary men, that ye will weary my G-d also? | [13] And he said, Hear ye now, O house of David; Is it a small thing for you to weary men, but will ye weary my God also? |
| 14: Therefore, the L-rd Himself shall give you a sign: behold, the young woman shall conceive, and bear a son, and shall call his name Immanuel. | [14] Therefore the Lord himself shall give you a sign; Behold, a virgin shall conceive, and bear a son, and shall call his name Immanuel. |
| 15: Curd and honey shall he eat, when he knoweth to refuse the evil, and choose the good. | [15] Butter and honey shall he eat, that he may know to refuse the evil, and choose the good. |
| 16: Yea, before the child shall know to refuse the evil, and choose the good, the land whose two kings thou hast a horror of shall be forsaken | [16] For before the child shall know to refuse the evil, and choose the good, the land that thou abhorrest shall be forsaken of both her kings. |

## The Concept of the Trinity Is Not Biblical

It is obvious these verses do not tell us the child named Immanuel is God in the flesh. The child is the sign that God will be with the House of David (in spirit) to dispose of their enemies. His name conveyed that message. The task, in fact, will be completed before the child is even old enough to make his own decisions concerning good and evil. Could that child be God? No. Again, God gave the child as a sign, and his name as a message (vs. 14). The child was not God.

The Disciples (and Jesus) taught from, and quoted scripture from the OT. Those were the complete scripture at the time of Jesus's life on Earth. The NT scriptures were written after Jesus's return to heaven. Therefore, when Matthew quoted Isaiah 7:14 (from the Septuagint) he was teaching that the whole situation of Mary's virgin pregnancy was a sign God is with the Jews even in their current situation. The Jewish people understood his message the same way the Hebrews understood the massage from Isaiah. It was the Roman Christians who made the decision to change that understanding. After they officially said Jesus was God (Council of Nicaea, 325 A.D.), Matthew 1:23 was one of the verses chosen to support their decision. They then took Isaiah 7:14, out of context, to justify the use of Matthew 1:23. Neither of these verses is meant to say, or even insinuate, Jesus is God in the flesh. The Roman Catholic Church, however, needed that to be the meaning.

More evidence this is the correct understanding comes from the fact Joseph was told "thou shalt call his name Jesus: for he shall save his people from their sins." (Matthew 1:21b) Many ask the question why the name Immanuel was quoted but the name Jesus was given. The answer is pretty simple. With the proper understanding of the quote, it is easy to see the name Immanuel was used in the teaching of a lesson. All of this is being done to show God is still with us through our troubles and despite our faults. That was the lesson taught in Isaiah. That same lesson applies to us today. The name Jesus was given to show His purpose for being born.

The name Jesus actually means "the Lord is salvation." As the angel told Joseph, He was given that name because saving His people from the penalty of sin is why He was sent. No, the two names are not interchangeable as some church leaders teach. They have different meanings. They convey different messages.

Isaiah 7:14 – is not a statement of prophesy of Jesus's birth. It, as well as Matthew 1:23, is a statement that God gives us signs that He is with us (Immanuel, Emmanuel) even as we fight our enemies. The enemies in Isaiah God defeated and saved the House of David from, through the sign of Immanuel, were men. The enemies God saved use from, through His Son Jesus, are the penalties for our sins. Neither name, Immanuel, or Jesus, means God in the flesh.

More chosen verses.

*Romans 9:5 Whose are the fathers, and of whom as concerning the flesh Christ came, who is over all, God blessed forever. Amen.*

This verse simply says Jesus is Blessed by God forever. In the preceding verse Paul talked about his ancestors who received the covenants and other things from God. (vs, 9:4) "the people of Israel. Theirs is the adoption to sonship; theirs the divine glory, the covenants, the receiving of the law, the temple worship and the promises." Verse 5 tells us those ancestors are the Father's people. Paul then says Jesus was born in the flesh from among those very people. He lets us know Jesus has been given authority over all (who is over all), and is forever Blessed by God. Nothing about this verse, when read in context to get the proper understanding, even hints that Jesus is God.

*Colossians 2:9 For in him dwelleth all the fulness of the Godhead bodily.*

This verse must be read in context beginning with verse 8. "Beware lest any man spoil you through philosophy and vain deceit, after the tradition of men, after the rudiments of the world, and not after Christ." Reading verse 9 out of context does not give the full idea being discussed. Verse 8 warns against being spoiled by the things of the world and not Christ. Verse 9 then tells us all of the things we look for in God we can get through Christ who was physically with us. The two verses, together, tell us we do not need philosophy, vain deceit, the tradition of men, or the rudiments of the world to get the spiritual fulfillment we seek.

We can get it all through Christ. The verses do not say that Christ is God. Verses 9 should be read with the same understanding as John 5:30. "I can of mine own self do nothing: as I hear, I judge: and my judgment is just; because I seek not mine own will, but the will of the Father which hath sent me." That is how the fulness of God dwells in Jesus Christ. Jesus does only the will of the Father. Jesus does all that the Father wills him to do. That is the fullness.

*Hebrews 1:8 – But unto the Son he saith, Thy throne, O God, is for ever and ever: a sceptre of righteousness is the sceptre of the kingdom.*

We have already discussed this verse in depth in the previous section. Another example of a verses that must be read in context.

*1 John 5:20 And we know that the Son of God is come, and hath given us an understanding, that we may know him that is true, and we are in him that is true, even in his Son Jesus Christ. This is the true God, and eternal life.*

It is curious why this verse is used in this section. Jesus is twice called the Son of God. It should be easy to realize the pronouns "him" and "his" refer directly to God (the Father). We may know him (God) that is true. We are in him (God) that is true. Even in His (God's) Son Jesus Christ. As a matter of fact, it is the Son of God (Jesus Christ) who came and gave us that understanding. It would be ridicules to interpret the last phrase to say, even in his (Jesus's) Son Jesus Christ. The last sentence in the verse sums it all up by saying the "him" that is true, the "him" we are in, and the one of whom Jesus is "his" son is the true God. That sentence is not calling "his" Son the true God. It will only be interpreted that way if you were first taught Jesus is God.

*1 John 3:16 – Hereby perceive we the love of God, because he laid down his life for us: and we ought to lay down our lives for the brethren*

Sometimes the addition of a single word or phrase can change the meaning of a verse. It can be difficult to know whether the addition was deliberate or not. How can you tell a word or phrase has been added? The addition may cause the meaning of a verse to conflict with other verses in scripture. This verse in the KJV seems to tell us God laid down His life for us. We know Jesus is the one who carried out that act. Those two statements imply Jesus is God. To find the true meaning of this verse two thing must be accomplished. We must identify the words that appear to be added and may have changed the meaning. We must also identify who is "he" that laid down his life for us.

The easiest way to identify the added words is to read the verse in various translations. Are there words that only appears in one translation and appears to change the meaning of the verse? Let's take a look.

- KJV – Hereby perceive we the love of God, because he laid down his life for us: and we ought to lay down our lives for the brethren.
- NIV – This is how we know what love is: Jesus Christ laid down his life for us. And we ought to lay down our lives for our brothers and sisters.
- NASB – We know love by this, that He laid down His life for us; and we ought to lay down our lives for the brothers and sisters.
- NLT – We know what real love is because Jesus gave up his life for us. So we also ought to give up our lives for our brothers and sisters.
- ESV – By this we know love, that he laid down his life for us, and we ought to lay down our lives for the brothers.

The words that seem to stand out and have an immediate influence on the meaning of the verse are "of God" in the KJV. Because we all want to have the love of God, it seems perfectly fine and natural for the verse to read as it does. There are two ways the additional words may be noticed. Read the verse in context. Read several translations of the same verse. Each translation has some differences in word choice. That should be expected. That only presents a problem when the word choice changes the meaning of the verse. Whether the change is intentional or not is the question.

Who is "he"? This is another case where the verse should not be read out of context. The KJV implies "he" is God. "...love of God, because he..." Two of the others (NIV and NLT) directly translate the "he" as Jesus. The "he" that laid down his life is identified back in verse 8. "He that committeth sin is of the devil; for the devil sinneth from the beginning. For this purpose, the Son of God was manifested, that he might destroy the works of the devil." We all know Jesus is the Son of God (Matthew 3:17, Luke 9:35, etc.). It does not matter from which translation you read verse 16, the "he" who "laid down his life" must be understood to be Jesus. We know that truth from all of the gospels. The insertion "of God" almost seems to be deliberate.

Ironically, with the proper understanding Jesus, the Son of God, is who the "he" is, the KJV is not totally incorrect. It was because of God's love that He gave His only begotten son for us (John 3:16) Therefore the change in meaning really comes from Trinity teaching, not necessarily the words alone. But we must wonder, were the words added for the purpose of aiding the Trinity teaching?

*John 14:9 – Jesus saith unto him, Have I been so long time with you, and yet hast thou not known me, Philip? he that hath seen me hath seen the Father; and how sayest thou then, Show us the Father?*

John 14:9 – is another verse that is often read alone. During the reading, emphases is put on the phrase "he that hath seen me hath seen the Father." This is interpreted to mean Jesus is saying, "the Father and I are the same," or are one. To understand the true meaning of that phrase the simple thing to do is continue reading through verse 10. "Believest thou not that I am in the Father, and the Father in me? the words that I speak unto you I speak not of myself: but the Father that dwelleth in me, he doeth the works."

Jesus says outright He does not speak of Himself. He speaks about the Father. (Re-read John 5:30) That tells us the interpretation of them being one is incorrect. The statement they are "in" each other is saying Jesus is doing only the will of the Father (God) and the Father is the one giving Him the directions. Jesus finishes by saying God (the Father) is the one that does the works. Jesus does not even take credit for Himself for the works the disciples have witnessed. He does not claim to be God. Why should we make that claim?

*John 10:30 – I and my Father are one*

The verse from John 10:30 is another verse Trinity teachers would have you read out of context. This verse is often quoted when the question is asked, "Who does Jesus say He is?" The answer that is given is, "this verse is Jesus saying He and the Father are the same spiritual being." Of course, that is followed by saying the Father is God. Since Jesus and the Father are one, then Jesus is saying He is God. Actually, when Jesus said who He is He said, "I am the Son of God."

Instead of reading only the one verse let us take a look at the entire conversation in which the statement was made. We must read beginning at verse 24 and continuing through verse 36 to get the full and accurate story.

*²⁴ Then came the Jews round about him, and said unto him, How long dost thou make us to doubt? If thou be the Christ, tell us plainly. ²⁵ Jesus answered them, I told you, and ye believed not: the works that I do in my Father's name, they bear witness of me. ²⁶ But ye believe not, because ye are not of my sheep, as I said unto you. ²⁷ My sheep hear my voice, and I know them, and they follow me: ²⁸ And I give unto them eternal life; and they shall never perish, neither shall any man pluck them out of my hand. ²⁹ My Father, which gave them me, is greater than all; and no man is able to pluck them out of my Father's hand. ³⁰ I and my Father are one. ³¹ Then the Jews took up stones again to stone him. ³² Jesus answered them, Many good works have I shewed you from my Father; for which of those works do ye stone me? ³³ The Jews answered him, saying, For a good work we stone thee not; but for blasphemy; and because that thou, being a man, makest thyself God.³⁴ Jesus answered them, Is it not written in your law, I said, Ye are gods? ³⁵ If he called them gods, unto whom the word of*

*God came, and the scripture cannot be broken;* [36] *Say ye of him, whom the Father hath sanctified, and sent into the world, Thou blasphemest; because I said, I am the Son of God?*

The conversation started with the Jewish leaders confronting Jesus to get Him to say He was the Christ. Throughout the conversation Jesus repeatedly referred to His Father (vs. 25, 29, 32). Even the miracles the Jews had witnessed, Jesus gave the credit to His Father (vs. 25). If Jesus wanted to call himself God, He could have taken the credit for Himself. He said His Father "is greater than all" (vs. 29). Can a person be greater than themselves? If Jesus and the Holy Spirit were fully God then neither would be greater than the other. That would be true even if they fulfilled different roles.

If one is greater than the other two then the two cannot be "fully" equal to the one. Since the Father is greater than all, then only the Father is God. When you say Jesus and the Holy Spirit are "fully" God, you say Jesus is lying when He said, "My Father … is greater than all."

The chosen verse was the conclusion of the statement Jesus made about His sheep. He said no man can take His sheep from him because His Father, who is greater than all, gave them to Him. Since you are not able to take anything from God, you cannot take from Me what God has given Me. God gave them to Me so I can give them eternal life (vs. 28) When it comes to protecting and providing for My sheep, "I and my Father are one" (in purpose). They are both protective of His sheep. The Jews took offense to Jesus's statement, because of their erroneous understanding, and accused Him of blasphemy for making Himself God. Jesus showed them the hypocrisy of their accusation by quoting from scripture (Psalms 82:6). He said their law makes the statement "I said, Ye are gods" and you accuse Me of blasphemy because "I said, I am the Son of God."

If a person has read this entire passage and still uses verse 30 to teach Jesus (the Son) is God, they are deliberately giving a false understanding of Jesus's words. The Jews accused Jesus of making Himself God. Jesus never said He was God. If he even wanted to make that claim, He could have used the quoted verse from Psalms to justify saying such. Yet, Jesus made the direct statement that He is the "Son of God" (vs. 36). The answer to the question "Who does Jesus say He is?" is right there. Again, Jesus said He is the "Son of God" (vs. 36). For man to say otherwise is turning the truth into a lie.

*John 1:1 – In the beginning was the Word, and the Word was with God, and the Word was God.*

*John 1:14 – And the Word was made flesh, and dwelt among us, (and we beheld his glory, the glory as of the only begotten of the Father,) full of grace and truth*

There are times when one is attempting to properly interpret and understand scripture it becomes necessary to do a word study. A word study is definitely necessary to understand the chosen verses from John 1. These two verses are the most convincing argument used to say Jesus is God. That statement is based on joining phrases taken from the two chosen verses: "…the Word was God…" and "…the Word was made flesh…." We all agree Jesus is the one from the heavenly realm who was made flesh. Therefore, calling Him the Word then saying the Word was God makes Jesus to be God. However, to get a clear and accurate understanding of the passage, it is necessary to truly understand the definition and usage of the actual term which is translated "the Word." The meaning and application must be taken from the time John penned his book. That would be close to three hundred years before the concepts of God the Son and the Trinity were infused into Christianity.

The term John used, that has been translated "the word," is "logos." Logos was primarily considered a Greek term at the time of the writing. History teaches us the NT was originally written in Greek. However, there was also a Hebrew usage of the term. That is why John felt it to be appropriate for use. In chapter 1, John was giving a summary of how the man Jesus qualified, and had the authority, to call Himself the Son of God. The religious leaders of the day felt it was blasphemy for Jesus to make such a claim. Yet, they did believe in the power of God and OT prophecies. John was telling the people, by God's inspiration, that the man, Jesus, came to us by God's power.

The definition of logos in the Greek is: the divine wisdom; reason; reasoned discourse. It is derived from the Greek word legein; to speak. In Hellenistic Judaism it would be translated "the uttered word." In ancient Greek literature it was used to express "the rational principle that governs and develops the universe." The ancient Greeks were not necessarily referring to our God, but that is the connotation in which John was inspired to use that word. Therefore, when logos is translated to say "the Word," it means "God's divine wisdom and reasoning that comes with the power of His spoken (uttered) WORD." That is the way it was understood until the creators of the Trinity creed found a need to justify their new teaching.

A few things to note: John penned these words a long time before the pagan concept of the Trinity was applied to Christianity. John walked with Jesus. The Roman Empire did not fully accept Christianity until about three-hundred years later. God and His sons (Job 1:6) existed in the spiritual realm before the creation of the physical (let us). The spirit son who became (was begotten) the man Jesus was among them. Yet, only one of the spirits was the Father. He is the one we call God (1 Corinthians 8:6) who is greater than all (John 10:29). Also remember, the interpretation of God inspired scripture cannot conflict with, or contradict, itself.

Now let's take a close look at the passage from John chapter one. We will not only read verses 1 and 14, we will read verses 1 through 18. Again, reading verses in context is important.

*The Study of John 1:1–18*

In the discussion and teaching of The Trinity the first chapter of John has become the strongest argument in support of the doctrine. More specifically, verses one and fourteen are the two verses singled out to teach the concept that Jesus is God. After the decision was made at the Council of Nicaea to call Jesus God, these two verses were deliberately separated out and interpreted to teach what would be the official creed of the new official Roman religion. The Holy Spirit was not included as God in the initial creed. The task was to convince the people God had walked this Earth in the person of Jesus. Roman citizens who chose to follow the emperor's new official religion had a man-god to worship.

It is important to establish a strong foundation before we discuss in detail the chosen verses and how they are used to support the doctrine. The first thing we must agree on is that the Word of God cannot contradict itself. 2 Timothy 3:16 tells us "All scripture is given by inspiration of God, and is profitable for doctrine, for reproof, for correction, for instruction in righteousness." This is probably the most important verse of scripture in the Bible. The truth of this verse is what establishes scripture as "The Word of God." Since God inspired it all, if the interpretation of a verse creates a conflict with another verse, at least one of the verses must have been interpreted incorrectly.

We also must remember John penned his Gospel in the first century AD. The Roman Emperor and the Council did not apply the concept of the Trinity until the fourth century. This is important because when you look at interpretations of scripture the original script and intent of the writer must be considered. Those who walked with Jesus never referred to Him as God. John was one such person. Because Jesus never taught His disciples He was God,

John would not have referred to Him as such. In his writing, John was testifying (John 21:24) from his personal experience why it was not blaspheme for Jesus to say He was the Son of God. Blaspheme was the charge the Jewish leaders brought against Jesus. They said He made Himself God. John's intent was to show that the man who walked among us did, in fact, have a divine nature. However, His divinity was as a Son who was with God (the Father) from the beginning. That was the understanding of John chapter one for the approximate 275 years before the Romans needed a different interpretation and understanding.

With that in mind, we must pay attention to the meaning of the terms John used. We must also make sure the application does not cause a conflict with other verses of scripture. If a conflict does occur, reading the verses in context, as they are written, will prove (reproof) which interpretation is correct. Again, for the purpose of consistency only the King James Version (KJV) will be used to quote scripture. The KJV NT was translated directly from a Greek text that was available at that time. That does not make it perfect. There are errors. The Greek text used had been manipulated by the Roman Catholic Church. The translators may also have been influenced in some way by the English language Bibles they were using before King James commissioned them to do a new English translation. Their works would also most likely reflect some of what they had been previously taught and accepted. Remember, the Trinity doctrine had been taught for about 1300 years before the KJV was commissioned. Also, with only the one translation being used here, if any conflicts are exposed, they can only be attributed to incorrect interpretation of scripture, not differences in translations. While these possibilities of error seem to bring into question the use of the KJV, the expertise of the NT translators' ability to understand Greek text is still recognized. However, where a literal translation is necessary for clarity, a Greek to English translation tool will be used.

## The Concept of the Trinity Is Not Biblical

Let us begin the study.

*John 1:1 In the beginning...*

This beginning is the same as in Genesis 1:1. "In the beginning God created..." This is the point in time that everything we experience as having physical existence (matter) comes into being. God, the Spirit (John 4:24), has no beginning. The time of His existence is appropriately described as eternity past. His Sons (Job 1:6), who also exists as spirits, were also with Him before this point in time. The Son who would become flesh was in that group (1 Peter 1:20) "Who verily was foreordained before the foundation of the world, but was manifest in these last times for you," So, "the beginning" was the beginning of physical existence not spiritual existence.

*...was the Word...*

The Word – Logos The divine wisdom, reasoning, and the power to speak and make things happen existed in the beginning. God did not have to figure things out as He went along.

*...and the Word was with God...*

God (the Father) held, within Himself, the power of using His divine wisdom and reasoning to create ("God created"). All of matter was created by the power of His speaking (uttered word). He was in control.

*...and the Word was God.*

This is one instance where previous translations and teaching influenced the KJV translators. When translated directly from the Greek text without influence, the end of verse one should read "and God was the Word."

Ἐν ἀρχῇ ἦν ὁ Λόγος, καὶ ὁ Λόγος ἦν πρὸς τὸν Θεόν, καὶ Θεὸς ἦν ὁ Λόγος. At the beginning was the Word, and the Word was to God, and God was the Word.

In the correct order, this tells us God Himself was the very power of divine wisdom, reasoning, and spoken Word that created. The reasoned discourse came into play as He directed others in His realm to do works (Let us...)

This portion of the verse was translated in the current order because Trinity teaching had been accepted centuries before the KJV was translated. Knowing now the term logos is what has been translated "the word," you still should not read "Jesus" into the verse in either order. That particular eisegesis occurs when we are taught to read verse 14 first.

*John 1:2 The same...*

After understanding everything that was created was done so by God's wisdom, reasoning, and the power of His speech, this is the first reference to Jesus. Jesus is the one John was teaching the Jewish leaders to accept His divinity. This is another place where Trinity influence played a role in the translation. "The same" really should ...be simply translated "He."

Οὗτος ἦν ἐν ἀρχῇ πρὸς τὸν θεόν.
He was in the beginning to god.

John's gospel is his testimony to the... truth of who Jesus was. It was directed toward unbelievers. First, he established God's authority. Now he says "He" (Jesus). The beginning of the verse was previously translated "The same" because Trinity teachers had taught "the Word" to mean Jesus. By saying "The same" it automatically referred back to "the Word" in verse one. That again inferred Jesus was "the Word" and therefore is God. John was actually beginning a new statement. He was not referring to the previous verse. John was teaching the Jewish leaders about the divinity of Jesus. John was referring directly to Jesus when he said "He." Again, "the Word" refers to God's power, not Jesus.

*...was in the beginning with God.*

Jesus (He), the Spirit (one of the Sons), was with God in the beginning. God had sons with him, in the same form as He (spirit), in the beginning. That is the meaning of Philippians 2:6. "Who, being in the form of God, thought it not robbery to be equal with God" Jesus was equal in form, not authority. Note: It says "to be equal with" not "a part of." Again, "the beginning" is the beginning of physical existence. Verse 2 tells us He (Jesus) was with God when God created the physical. Jesus was with God before the foundation of the world. John 17:5 ⁵"And now, O Father, glorify thou me with thine own self with the glory which I had with thee before the world was". Also read 1 Peter 1:19–20. Jesus had glory with the Father before the world even was. "He" was in the beginning with God.

*John 1:3 – All things were made by him; and without him was not any thing made that was made.*

The important thing to note here is that things were "made" by (through) Jesus. There is a huge difference between creating and making. As stated in Genesis 1:1, "God Created." He and His Sons would have taken the physical material newly created and "made" it into what we observe. "And the earth was without form, and void…" (Genesis 1:2a) Scripture does not specifically say in Genesis who gave the Earth its form. John, however, was inspired to testify to it in verse 1:10. The verse we are looking at here does indicate Jesus (as spirit) was involved. When God spoke, using reasoned discourse, to the group (Genesis 1:26, "let us") it is clear others were involved in the "making" processes. The fact Jesus (as spirit) was present and involved in what was going on does not make Him God. "Us" is plural not singular. (Also see Genesis 3:22 and 11:7) Another indication "creating" and "making" are different actions is in the statement of what God rested from. "… he had rested from all his work which God created and made."

*John1:4 – In him was life; and the life was the light of men.*

In Jesus, and our faith and belief in Him, is the pathway to eternal life. The people of that day had gotten off of the path and did not even know it. Jesus was the shining light that would allow us to see the direction we needed to go. Believing in Him would light our way back to the right path.

*John 1:5 – And the light shineth in darkness; and the darkness comprehended it not*

This was intended to be a wake-up message to those who were leading the people in the wrong direction. Because the religious leaders had decided for themselves how the savior would come, they and their followers, did not recognize the illuminated fulfillment of prophesies right before them. They were in the dark. You are out on a dark, moonless night and you have already decided which way you are going. You trust those who are leading. You may not notice the light that is being shined on the correct path by the one you really should be following. Jesus's light was shining. They were trying to put it out.

*John 1:6 There was a man sent from God, whose name was John.*

Here John is informing/reminding the people the messenger they all knew (John the Baptist) {JtB} was sent by God. He was not just an ordinary person preaching his own message.

*John 1:7 The same came for a witness, to bear witness of the Light....*

The purpose of JtB's ministry was to forewarn the people that the savior they were waiting for was coming. The one coming would shine the light on the pathway for them to follow. JtB would identify the one who is the light. With that light they would be able to see the truth.

*...that all men through him might believe.*

In God's wisdom, He sent the messenger (JtB) so the people might believe the Messiah was coming. They had been waiting for him for four hundred years. Those who believed JtB would accept and believe in Jesus as the Messiah.

*John 1:8 – He was not that Light, but was sent to bear witness of that Light.*

When John penned his gospel, it was being written as a historical testimony of the things he knew and witnessed. Even though JtB had followers (disciples), he was not to be mistaken for the Messiah. The second part of his mission, after warning of the coming, JtB was to identify (bear witness of) the Messiah when He arrived.

*John 1:9 That was the true Light, which lighteth every man that cometh into the world.*

The one JtB identified as the Messiah (Jesus) was the true Messiah. The important word in this verse is "true." Jesus was the one who truly illuminated the path to salvation. Other cultures, including the Romans, had entities they worshipped as gods or saviors. Those others had shown no sign they actually had any divine abilities at all. Jesus had done so. The opportunity for salvation Jesus presented was offered to all men of the world (John 3:16).

*John 1:10 – He was in the world....*

This divine person who lighted our pathway to salvation lived in this world among us. He was a physical being.

*...and the world was made by him...*

This goes back to a statement made previously. Jesus, while He was still in the form of God (Philippians 2:6), was instrumental in taking the matter God created and doing the making. This is where we are told specifically the world (Earth) was made by Him. Until He did, "...the earth was without form...." (Genesis 1:2)

*...and the world knew him not.*

John was testifying that, as great as Jesus was, many of the people of the world (the religious leaders) still would not accept Him as the Messiah. For whatever reason they did not recognize him by the fulfillment of prophesy and did not believe the message given through JtB.

*John 1:11 – He came unto his own...*

The Hebrew people were God's chosen people. They knew God through scripture and historical experience. Jesus was born as one of these people. When He began His earthly ministry, He went straight to God's chosen people, His own heritage, first to teach and show them the pathway to salvation. He did not go directly to the other cultures of the world (gentiles).

*...and his own received him not.*

Sometimes when you feel you are ordinary, it is difficult to accept the fact someone great can come out of your group. That was the case with Jesus. We know your family. We played together growing up. Now you want us to believe you are the Messiah our people have been waiting four centuries for. Yea, right. You saying such things is blasphemy. Jesus addressed that issue directly in Mark 6:4. But Jesus, said unto them, A prophet is not without honor, but in his own country, and among his own kin, and in his own house

*John 1:12 – But as many as received him...*

This is an important verse because those who did receive Him consisted of both Jews and non-Jews (gentiles). Even some naturally born Roman citizens were in this group. The many people who heard and believed his messages are being pointed out.

*...to them gave he power to become the sons of God,*

even to them that believe on his name:
All who believe on Jesus receive the gift of salvation. As believers we are now considered by God to be His sons (and daughters) by adoption. (Romans 8:15). Notice the verse does not say those who receive Jesus became His sons. We become the sons of God (the Father).

*John 1:13 – Which were born, not of blood, nor of the will of the flesh, nor of the will of man, but of God.*

Jesus was not born by normal human biological means. He was not born from sexual desires and actions. He was not born because a man and woman decided to have a child. Jesus was born of God. God made the decision to have His Son born in the flesh to give us a pathway back to Him. It was by God's divine wisdom and reasoning how He would provide the opportunity for us to receive salvation. God chose to impregnate a virgin to make sure no man, not even Joseph, could claim Jesus as his own son.

*John 1:14 – And the Word was made flesh, and dwelt among us....*

God used His wisdom, reasoning, and power (Logos) (Word) to have His Son born of a virgin woman. It was all His idea. God knew man would continue to struggle to stay on the right path without a leader we could touch. He loved us and had the desire that we would be saved. So, it was by the power of His reasoning, His wisdom and His uttered word (logos) that Mary became pregnant. That is how God's Son, who existed in the spirit realm before the foundation of the Earth, was born (begotten) in the flesh. It all happened by God's Will; by God's Word. Mary is the virgin vessel God chose to have His logos become a man in the flesh.

This is the portion of verse fourteen Trinity teachers couple with verse one to teach Jesus is God. They use, "the Word became flesh" to identify "the Word" as Jesus. They then put the two verses together to say the man Jesus is God the Son. The remainder of this verse contradicts that claim. Of course, they deliberately omit, or ignore, the remainder of this verse. That oversight servs their purposes well. Knowing the true meaning of logos gives us the proper perspective to understand the entire verse.

## The Concept of the Trinity Is Not Biblical

*... (and we beheld his glory, the glory as of the only begotten of the Father) full of grace and truth.*

This clearly says God's Word was presented to us as "the only begotten of the Father." God had the desire for man to have a pathway by which he could be saved. He used His wisdom and reasoning to decide how, and His power to make it happen. "Begat" means to produce offspring. Jesus is the only offspring God produced through a woman. The man Jesus who lived in the flesh is the Son of God, not the second person of God. God did not begat another part of Himself. Sorry Catholic worshippers. Mary is not the mother of God. She is the mother of God's only begotten "Son."

To make Jesus become God the Son you must first ignore the true meaning of "the Word" (logos). Then take and read only the first part of verse fourteen, out of context, and use it to identify "the Word" as Jesus. Then go back and read verse one with the order of words as they are in current translations while inserting "Jesus" as the meaning/identification of "the word." During the process the description of Jesus as "the only begotten of the Father" has to be ignored. Is that how scripture should be read?

*John 1:15 – John bare witness of him, and cried, saying, This was he of whom I spake, He that cometh after me is preferred before me: for he was before me.*

This is the account of when JtB identified and introduced Jesus to the people. "...is preferred before me..." is JtB's way of saying Jesus is more important than himself.

We know from scripture that JtB was six months older than Jesus in the flesh. When he said Jesus "was before me" that is an indication Jesus existed in a different form (spirit) before being born in the flesh.

*John 1:16 – And of his fulness have all we received, and grace for grace.*

Because Jesus has come, we have the opportunity (grace) to live right and receive salvation rather than what we deserve. His fullness includes love, mercy, and grace. We have all received the gift (Ephesians 2:8b). Some of us have yet to open it.

*John 1:17 – For the law was given by Moses, but grace and truth came by Jesus Christ.*

The law we have found so difficult to keep was given to us by God through Moses, the writer of the Torah. Jesus, however, gives us another chance (grace) to follow the true pathway to salvation. Yes, we should make every effort to live right. However, if salvation depended on that we would never make it. No matter how hard we try, we all fall short (Romans 3:23). Thank God for the grace we receive through Jesus Christ.

*John 1:18 – No man hath seen God at any time, the only begotten Son, which is in the bosom of the Father, he hath declared him.*

John penned his testimony after Jesus (the only begotten Son) had returned to heaven to be with (in the bosom of) His Father (God). That makes this verse very important in the Trinity discussion. Jesus had lived among us and had been seen by many. This verse clearly tells us no man has seen God. The phrase "at any time" puts more emphasis on that point. Moses had very close encounters with God, but not even he saw God's face. (Exodus 33:20–25, 34:5–6) Simple logic: No man has seen God; men have seen Jesus; Jesus cannot be God. The same Jesus that has returned to be with the Father, had declared God's existence, His kingdom, and His desire for us to be with Him. He did all of this while He was with us in the flesh.

John wrote the first eighteen verses of his gospel to give a brief synopsis of the remainder of his testimony. He immediately began, in verse nineteen, to fill in the details. It was necessary to cover all eighteen verses in this discussion to give a clear picture of what the one-and-a-half chosen Trinity verses really say when read in context. Choosing only certain verses or parts of verses is a common practice when one wants to deceive another. The first part of verse 14 had to be taken first to identify the term "the Word" as Jesus. That was based solely on the phrase "was made flesh." They would have you ignore the remainder of the verse where Jesus is identified as "the only begotten of the Father." Then you are led backwards to read verse one. The order of the words in verse one was changed to give the concept they wanted us to believe. "God was the Word" was changed to say "the Word was God" The need to complete the claim, and be able to teach, that Jesus is the second person of God was fulfilled with these deceptions. The complete reading of verse 18 dispels all of that.

Summary: God (the Father) Himself was the power, wisdom, and reasoning, that created.; Jesus (and possibly His brothers) made everything into what we are able to observe, from God's created matter. Jesus formed the Earth. He was the source of the eternal life light but the people living in darkness could not see it. John the Baptist preached of the coming Messiah and introduced Him to the people. It is ironic that Jesus made the world but some of us did not recognize Him when He was here. His own people rejected the idea He could be the Messiah even after witnessing the fulfillment of prophesy. Those who did believe Him, Jews and Gentiles, became/become the sons of God, not the sons of Jesus. Jesus was not conceived by human biological means. He was conceived of God. God's decision how to offer us salvation, using His wisdom, reasoning, and power (logos), was manifested in the flesh. We beheld Him as the only begotten Son of the Father, not the second person of God. John the Baptist identified Jesus and taught of the grace we receive through Him. Since no man as seen God at any time, Jesus cannot be God. He was seen by men. The same man, Jesus, who had gone back to be with His Father before this gospel was written, had declared the truth of who God is while He was with us. Jesus never declared Himself to be God. Should we?

# Why We Should Not Teach Or Accept The Trinity As Doctrine

2 Timothy 3:16 must be mentioned again. We should definitely not want to contradict scripture that God inspired the disciples/apostles to write down. If such discrepancies are found that is the epitome of false teaching. It is difficult for us, as adults, to accept the fact something we have believed most of our lives is not the truth. However, we are warned several times in scripture to be aware of false prophets and teachers (Matthew 7:15, 1 Timothy 6:3–5). The problem is we tend to only look at the ones who are speaking during our lifetime. They are easy to identify. We do not look for those in the past. They are much harder to identify. As we are taught things growing up, we seldom, if ever, check to find out if we have been taught the truth. Because we trust the teacher, we trust what they have taught. On the subject of the Trinity, it is time to use scripture for reproof and correction.

In God's wisdom He anticipated the need for us to be taught again as adults some of the things we should have been taught correctly as children. That is why He had the writer of Hebrews to pen verse 5:12. For when for the time ye ought to be teachers, ye have need that one teach you again which be the first principles of the oracles of God; and are become such as have need of milk, and not of strong meat. As believers in God, and his Word, it is time to apply this verse.

Hebrews 5:12 tells us we, adults, have need to be taught the very basics of our faith (have need of milk). The most basic concept to be relearned is "the Bible is the Word of God." We can make that statement, and believe it with true faith, because of 2 Timothy 3:16. If we are going to re-teach the very basics about who God is, and why we should have faith in Him, the information must be taken solely from the only textbook He Himself inspired the writing of. Remember, we are talking about the milk not the meat. Because we identify our faith as Christianity, we must use the same source when we re-teach who the CHRIST is. Most importantly we must use exegesis (taking information from what is written) not eisegesis (reading into the text what we what it to say).

The teaching of the Trinity has adversely affected how we respond to the written Word of God. In the Great Commission, given by Jesus, we are told to teach, "...them to observe all things whatsoever I have commanded you...." Jesus commanded us to pray to the Father in His name. The Trinity tells us we can ignore that. We are told, with Jesus being God we do not have to pray to the Father only. We can pray directly to Him. Because we have decided He is God, we have also decided we can ignore who He told us to pray to. Jesus did not tell us to pray to God. He said pray to the Father. Even if you believe in the Trinity, you are still violating Jesus's instructions if you pray to Him. There have been many prayers where the names Father and Jesus have been used interchangeably in the same prayer. That is not proper.

God inspired the writing of the scripture that tells us, "but to us there is one God, the Father..." The Trinity calls God a liar saying "no," to us there is really one God, the Father, the Son, and the Holy Spirit. God tells us in His Word, "For there are three that testify: 8 the[a] Spirit, the water and the blood; and the three are in agreement." The Trinity tells us God does not know the whole story. We are going to tell God the story should say, "For there are three that bear record in heaven, the Father, the Word, and the Holy

*The Concept of the Trinity Is Not Biblical*

Ghost: and these three are one. ⁸And there are three that bear witness in earth, the Spirit, and the water, and the blood: and these three agree in one." We are taught in scripture to worship God (John 4:23, Luke 4:8, Hebrews 12:28, etc.) John 4:23 talks about true worshipers. Even Jesus said, "… Thou shalt worship the Lord thy God, and him only shalt thou serve." The Trinity tells us, by rationalizing, it is OK to worship Jesus and the Holy Spirit. That is actually written in the creed. Many churches have graven images and what would be considered likenesses of Jesus in their buildings. They rationalize they are not violating God's commandment against such because Jesus is God. They say God could not have meant do not have any graven images or likenesses of Himself.

Because we think we are smart enough to decide who is God, we also think we can say what God meant when He inspired the writing of scripture. Wrong again. For my thoughts are not your thoughts, neither are your ways my ways, saith the LORD.⁹ For as the heavens are higher than the earth, so are my ways higher than your ways, and my thoughts than your thoughts. (Isaiah 55:8–9) We should not even pretend to understand anything about God over what is written.

It has already been shown that the chosen Trinity verses, when read objectively and in context, do not say what we are most commonly taught. Instead of continuing to disprove what we have been taught certain verses to say, let's read a few verses again for the first time (milk).

**Why we should not teach or believe in "God the Son."**

1 Corinthians 8:6a teaches us, "But to us there is but one God, the Father… Part b of the same verse teaches us, "… and one Lord Jesus Christ…." When it comes to "milk" teaching we learn from this verse God is the Father and Jesus is the Christ. "to us" they are to be two separate persons fulfilling two sperate roles in our lives. Why do we refer to God as the Father? When God spoke

about who Jesus is He said in Matthew 3:17b, "This is my beloved Son, in whom I am well pleased." That statement from God makes Him the Father and Jesus the Son. Again, if we are not to contradict God, we are to teach the Father (God) is a separate person from the Son (Jesus). If we teach "God the Son" we directly contradict God's inspired Word. By doing so, we contradict God. If we teach that "to us" there is but one God, The Father, the Son, and the Holy Spirit, we are telling God what He really meant when He inspired 1 Corinthians 8:6.

If certain verses of scripture are interpreted in such a way they create a contradiction with other verses, or more importantly with what God has said, even a "milk" learner should feel something is not right.

The basic "milk" of Jesus's own words teaches us the Father (God) is the one running things, not He Himself (the Son). John 12:49 For I have not spoken of myself; but the Father which sent me, he gave me a commandment, what I should say, and what I should speak. John 5:30 I can of mine own self do nothing: as I hear, I judge: and my judgment is just; because I seek not mine own will, but the will of the Father which hath sent me. If Jesus is the second person of the one God, why does He repeatedly say the Father sent Him? He could have said, "I just decided to come." If they are two persons within the one God, would one person have more authority than the other? Everything Jesus spoke and did was at the Father's (God's) will, not His own. To make it perfectly clear, Jesus actually said at the beginning of verse 12:49 (referring to previous verses {46–48} about who would judge non-believers in the last days) that He was not talking about Himself. There are many other verses in scripture with the same message. Please do not contradict Jesus. When Jesus did talk about Himself, He said, "I am the son of God." (John 10:36) Stop trying to camouflage this simple "milk" as "strong meat" by saying Jesus being both the Son and God at the same time is a mystery that is hard to explain. Neither God nor Jesus makes that claim. It is simply not true.

The Word of God tells us even when Jesus returned to heaven He did not "become God again." They are still separate persons. Jesus did not become God's right hand. He was sat at the right hand of God. Here are just a few of the many scripture verses that teach us that very thing.

*Romans 8:34 – It is Christ that died, yea rather, that is risen again, who is even at the right hand of God....*

*1 Peter 3:21b-22a – ...by the resurrection of Jesus Christ: ²²Who is gone into heaven, and is on the right hand of God...*

*Mark 16:19 – ¹⁹So then after the LORD had spoken unto them, he was received up into heaven, and sat on the right hand of God.*

When these verses are read in context, it becomes even more evident that when God inspired the writing of scripture, He never showed Jesus to be a part of Himself. When the following passage from Ephesians is read it should be impossible for anyone who believes the Bible to be the Word of God to say God and Jesus are one.

*Ephesians 1:17–20 That the God of our Lord Jesus Christ, the Father of glory, may give unto you the spirit of wisdom and revelation in the knowledge of him: ¹⁸ The eyes of your understanding being enlightened; that ye may know what is the hope of his calling, and what the riches of the glory of his inheritance in the saints, ¹⁹ And what is the exceeding greatness of his power to us-ward who believe, according to the working of his mighty power, ²⁰ Which he wrought in Christ, when he raised him from the dead, and set him at his own right hand in the heavenly places....*

This passage starts by telling us the Father of glory is also the God "of" Jesus. The teaching of the Trinity, and the way they interpret other verses, directly contradict this. If they were two parts of one, neither could be the God "of" the other. The passage ends by telling us God, Himself, set Jesus at His right hand. The practice of para-phrasing could have been used to make the point "that the God of our Lord Jesus Christ, the Father of glory… set him at his own right hand in the heavenly places." It is important, though, to include the entire passage. The continuity of the verses leaves no doubt that it was God the Father who set Jesus at His right hand. You should not believe they are two persons within one.

**Why you should not believe in "God the Holy Spirit"**

Knowing now that Jesus (the Son) is not God, the Trinity cannot be a true doctrine. However, because the Holy Spirit is included in the false teaching, we must discuss it here.

Although it has been shown the chosen Trinity teaching verses do not say what the teachers tell you, it is important to discuss this from the Bible first view. This can be difficult because, in Trinity teaching, several terms are used as if they are interchangeable. Trinity teachers would have you believe God is the only person who exists in the spirit form. They want you to accept the terms Holy Ghost, Holy Spirit, Spirit of God, and other names of spirits are all referring to the same spirit; God. Let's see what scripture actually says.

Jesus even said there was a time He was in the same form as God. Let this mind be in you, which was also in Christ Jesus: [6]Who, being in the form of God, thought it not robbery to be equal with God: [7]But made himself of no reputation, and took upon him the form of a servant, and was made in the likeness of men: (Philippians 2:5–7) It would not have been necessary to make the comparison of being equal in form (spirit) if the two were the same one. Of course, being equal in form does not mean equal in position. The Father is the Lord of the Son and the others who exists in the spirit realm.

To overcome the hurdle of multiple names for spirits it is imperative that we pay close attention to function of the named spirit in our lives. Of course, the discussion is whether or not the Holy Spirit is God. We will look for statements that indicate separation of unity. The following set of verses will distinguish the spirit that we call the Holy Spirit in this conversation.

> *John 14:15–17a – [15]If ye love me, keep my commandments. [16]And I will pray the Father, and he shall give you another Comforter, that he may abide with you for ever; [17]Even the Spirit of truth; whom the world cannot receive...*

> *John 14:26 – [26]But the Comforter, which is the Holy Ghost, whom the Father will send in my name, he shall teach you all things, and bring all things to your remembrance, whatsoever I have said unto you.*

> *John 16:12–13 – [12]I have yet many things to say unto you, but ye cannot bear them now. [13]Howbeit when he, the Spirit of truth, is come, he will guide you into all truth: for he shall not speak of himself; but whatsoever he shall hear, that shall he speak: and he will shew you things to come.*

Here the Holy Spirit is called by three different names: the Comforter, the Spirit of Truth, and the Holy Ghost. His function in our lives is to teach or guide us to the truth. The Father (God) is the one who is sending the spirit. Notice the scripture does not say God is sending another part of Himself or another God. Please do not read that into the verses because you were taught that before you read the verses for yourself. Verse 14:16 names all three persons and in no way insinuates they are each a part of one. We are told the Father will "give" us another comforter. It does not say another comforter will decide to come down.

Just as with Jesus, there is an indication the Holy Spirit is not God. Verse 16:13 tells us "he shall not speak of himself." The truth he will guide us to will be given to him by God (the Father). If the Holy Spirit was a person of Gid he would be able to speak of himself. He would not have to hear from another source. If He (or Jesus) is God and is speaking only what God tells him but is not speaking of himself that would be a classic oxymoron. That type of internal conflict or contradiction cannot exist in scripture inspired by the one true God (the Father). Trying to explain it away by calling it a mystery is not acceptable. He shall not speak for himself because God (the Father) is who He shall hear from. What he hears from the Father (God) is what He will speak. The Holy Spirit is not God.

# Conclusion

"But to us there is one God, the Father..." When you say there is one God, the Father, the son, and the Holy Spirit, you have changed the truth into a fable 2 Timothy 4:3–4 *For the time will come when they will not endure sound doctrine; but after their own lusts shall they heap to themselves teachers, having itching ears; And they shall turn away their ears from the truth, and shall be turned unto fables.* Making the change from their pagan religions to Christianity created a religious divide within the Roman Empire. The Roman Emperor and other religious leaders had their own lust of wanting unity restored within the empire as they formed their Catholic Church. That included pacifying both polytheistic and monotheistic worshipers. They applied the pagan fable that one can also be three. Because Roman citizens grew up being taught the concepts of the Trinity, that is the very fable their itching ears were listening for. They wanted to hear it said Jesus is God. The creed created by men was just the outline for the fable.

God repeatedly called Jesus His Son. Jesus repeatedly called God His Father. God is a Spirit... (John 4:24a). Jesus was also a spirit until, by God's "Word," He was begotten of a virgin and born in the flesh. Philippians 2:6–8 *[6]Who, being in the form of God, thought it not robbery to be equal with God: [7]But made himself of no reputation, and took upon him the form of a servant, and was made in the likeness of men.* If being formerly in spirit form made Him God there would have been no reason to make a statement of equality. Also, the verse says "...being in the form of God...." It does not say "being God" or "a person of God." There is no verse in scripture that actually says Jesus is God. Trinity teacher do, however, interpret certain verses in a way to seem to make that statement.

The Holy Spirit at various times carries the titles Holy Ghost, Spirit of Truth. Comforter, and Spirit of God. Neither of these titles, including Spirit of God, Says the Holy Spirit is God. Should the seven Spirits of God mentioned in Revelation (1:4; 3:1; 4:5; 5:6) all be considered God simply by title alone? There is no verse in scripture that says the Holy Spirit, the Spirit of God, or any spirit by any other name is God except himself. The teaching that the Holy Spirit is God comes from the use of extra-scriptural information; the revised creed. Although God Himself is described as being a Spirit (John 4:24), that does not make every spirit God.

The only person that scripture directly says is God is the Father. Because of the influence of Trinity teaching, there are a few verses that seem to infer the Son is God. However, when they are read in context with a full explanation the truth is revealed. The Son is only doing the will of the one who sent Him, the Father. If the Son is God, why can He not speak for Himself? The same question applies to the Holy Spirit. The bottom line is, The Trinity is not sound doctrine. Knowing true doctrine is profited from God inspired scripture (2 Timothy 3:16), the Trinity should not be considered doctrine at all. It is pagan religious tradition instilled into the Christian religion by the framers of the Roman Catholic Church.

Despite the number of scriptures that were quoted and discussed in this study, many people will not accept the truth that is revealed. They will question how a false doctrine could have been taught and accepted for so many centuries. The answer comes in two parts. 1) The doctrine was crafted during the formation of the

## The Concept of the Trinity Is Not Biblical

Roman Catholic Church. The Roman Empire was in control of religious matters for over a thousand years before the Empire was dissolved. The Roman Catholic Church influenced religious teaching throughout all of Europe. Even during the period of reformation many Catholic teachings were not questioned. 2) Most religious leaders do not actually apply 1 Timothy 2:15 to this topic. *Study to shew thyself approved unto God, a workman that needeth not to be ashamed, rightly dividing the word of truth.* Unfortunately, the typical method of Christian education is just to repeat what you have been taught. We simply accept what we are told by the Pastor, Priest, or Professor. No one in modern history has questioned whether or not "the Word" really refers directly to Jesus. It is taught because that is what was learned. Now is the time to apply Hebrews 5:12.

The Trinity is a false doctrine adopted to settle a dispute and make the new official Roman religion acceptable to all of the Roman citizens.

The truth: The Father is the ONE GOD. Jesus is the SON OF GOD, the CHRIST, and our LORD. The Holy Spirit is our COMFORTER and the SPIRIT OF TRUTH. That is who the Holy Scripture says they are "to us" (1 Corinthians 8:6). The concept of the Trinity was adopted into the Christian religion by the Roman Catholic Church from a previous Roman pagan religion. THE THREE PERSONS ARE NOT ALL A PART OF ONE GOD. AMEN.